ABOUT THE AUTHOR

Moustafa Gadalla was born in Cairo, Egypt in 1944. He graduated from Cairo University with a Bachelor of Science in civil engineering in 1967. He immigrated to the U.S.A. in 1971 and continued to practice engineering as a licensed professional engineer and land surveyor. He is an independent Egyptologist who spent most of his adult life studying, and researching scores of books about Egyptology, mythology, religions, the Bible, languages, etc.

He is the author of six internationally-acclaimed books about ancient Egypt. He is the chairman of the Tehuti Research Foundation, an international, U.S.-based, non-profit organization, dedicated to ancient Egyptian studies.

OTHER BOOKS BY THE AUTHOR

Historical Deception
The Untold Story of Ancient Egypt (2nd Ed.)
ISBN: 0-9652509-2-X (pbk.), 352 pages, US$19.95

Egyptian Cosmology: The Absolute Harmony
ISBN: 0-9652509-1-1 (pbk.), 160 pages, US$9.95

Egyptian Harmony: The Visual Music
ISBN: 0-9652509-8-9 (pbk.), 192 pages, US$11.95

Exiled Egyptians: The Heart of Africa
ISBN: 0-9652509-6-2 (pbk.), 352 pages, US$19.95

Egypt: A Practical Guide
ISBN: 0-9652509-3-0 (pbk.), 256 pages, US$8.50

Tut-Ankh-Amen: The Living Image of the Lord
ISBN: 0-9652509-9-7 (pbk.), 144 pages, US$9.50

To my wife and soulmate, Faith,
a fountain of warmth and love.

Testimonials for the First Edition
(original title: **Pyramid Illusions: A Journey to the Truth**)

Midwest Book Review - 3/97 - Jim Cox

Pyramid Illusions challenges the common theories about the Egyptian stone pyramids. Pyramid Illusions is a culmination of original research, imaginative writing, and many useful illustrations to help the reader envision him/herself at the sites and interiors of the Egyptian masonry pyramids. Controversial, articulate, challenging, Pyramid Illusions is a fascinating contribution to Egyptology.

Saxton Book Reviews - 3/97 - Jon Baughman

Pyramid Illusions is a book about the pyramids -- not just the great pyramids, but other known pyramids in Egypt. Gadalla takes a new, fresh look at their possible uses and their construction. His viewpoints go against conventional lines of thought.

...you will find this book very interesting.

The Independent Review - 1/98 - Armidale, Australia

Gadalla has allowed history to speak for itself through physical evidence, historical documents and primary materials...Gadalla at the same time is an easy to read, pragmatic author. He writes in small sections, uses charts, points and illustrations so that his book is of value to both those with a cursory interest and the professional.

Book Cover Artwork by K&D Design, North East, PA, USA

PYRAMID HANDBOOK

Second Edition, Revised

Moustafa Gadalla

Maa Kheru *(True of Voice)*

Tehuti Research Foundation
International Head Office: Greensboro, NC, U.S.A.

Pyramid Handbook

by MOUSTAFA GADALLA

Published by:
Tehuti Research Foundation
P.O. Box 39406
Greensboro, NC   27438-9406, U.S.A.

This book is a revised and enhanced edition of the originally titled *Pyramid Illusions: A Journey to the Truth*, by Moustafa Gadalla. The name was changed to better reflect the content of the book, and to avoid the appearance of self-righteousness.

Publisher's Cataloging-in-Publication
(Provided by Quality Books, Inc.)

Gadalla, Moustafa, 1944-
    Pyramid handbook / by Moustafa Gadalla (Maa Kheru). -- 2nd ed., rev.
    p. cm.
    Includes bibliographical references and index.
    First ed. issued in 1997 under title Pyramid illusions.
    LCCN: 00-130200
    ISBN: 0-9652509-4-6

    1. Pyramids--Egypt. 2. Egypt--Antiquities. 3. Geometry--Philosophy. 4. Stone, Cast. 5. Masonry--Egypt--History.
I. Gadalla, Moustafa, 1944- Pyramid illusions. II. Title.

DT63.G24 2000   932
                               QBI00-26

Table of Contents

Overview

The Ten Pyramids

Giza

Abu Rawash

Giza

Epilogue

Appendixes

Preface

In a little over a century, the ancient Egyptians built ten masonry pyramids, which contained more than twenty five (25) million tons of limestone blocks.

Academia has confused and clouded the history of Egypt and its pyramids with misrepresentations, deceptions, and distortions. From a distance, what we have learned about the pyramids may appear factual, but once we examine it closer, it proves to be otherwise. This book is intended to undo many of the false perceptions about the ancient Egyptians' pyramids.

This book is a major overhaul of our previously published book, Pyramid Illusions: A Journey to the Truth, ISBN 0-9652509-7-0. The title of the new book, Pyramid Handbook, is more representative of its contents and material.

Both the subjects of harmonic proportions (sacred geometry) and the related functional objectives of the pyramids are addressed in this new book.

Join us on our journey to find the truth — the WHOLE truth — about the pyramids.

Read this book as an unbiased, fair juror.

Moustafa Gadalla
May, 2000

Standards and Terminology

1 -   We have gotten accustomed to repeating wrongly inter-
preted words and names, from the ancient Egyptian texts.
For example, the ancient Egyptian word **neter**, and its femi-
nine form **netert**, have been wrongly, and possibly intentionally, translated to *god* and *goddess*, by almost all academicians. There is no equivalent word in meaning, to the
word **neter**, in the English language. Honest translators
should use the native word, if they cannot find its equivalent in their language.

Neteru (plural of **neter/netert**) are the divine principles
and functions that operate the universe. They are all aspects and functions of the One Supreme God.
The words *god* and *goddess* leave the impression that ancient Egyptians had a multitude of *gods*, which is absolutely untrue.

2 -   The Greeks had a disdainful attitude to all non-Greek
names, and arbitrarily changed them. The Egyptian name
Tehuti, was rendered by the Greeks variously as Thoth,
Thouth, Thout. In theophoric [**neter** (god)-bearing] names
they introduced further corruption plus the ornament of
a Greek ending. It has become fashionable among many
modern academicians to use the Greek renderings of Egyptian names, in their translations.

When referring to the names of cities, Pharaohs, **neteru**
(gods/goddesses), etc., if the commonly used Greek name
is different than the true Egyptian name, we will show
the correct Egyptian name followed by the common, but
arbitrary Greek rendering between parentheses. Let us
be fair and get used to the correct names.

3 -   Throughout this book, fonting of quotations varies depending on the source of quotation. There are generally three types of fonting:

Δ   **The reader/traveler's questions, remarks, experiences are indicated in this special font.**

Δ The answers and explanations will be indicated in this particular font.

Δ   This font is reserved for background information.

Δ *This font is used to refer to ancient Egyptian sources.*

Δ   *This font is to refer to quotes from other sources.*

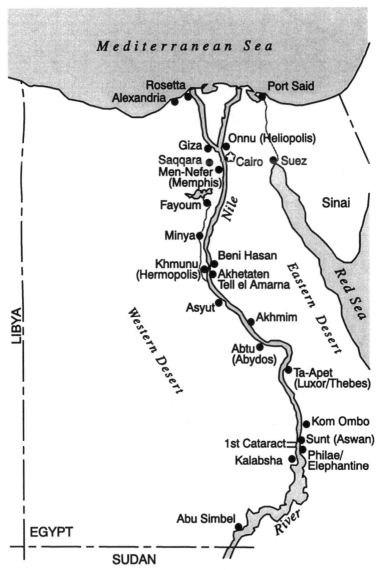

Egypt (Present-Day)

OVERVIEW

The Reader Travels

Imagine yourself, the reader, traveling to Egypt to view the sites of the pyramids. You already have prior information about the subject, based on what you have heard, read and seen. You may have some doubts, misconceptions and conflicting information, so you are eager to learn the truth.

When you travel now to Egypt, you are going there with an open mind. You are rational and willing to listen and evaluate. You may change prior views, if logic warrants it.

The author will guide you throughout your travels, and will present you with the facts and the fiction. He will clarify and sort out the various issues. But it is up to you to piece the puzzle together. By no means do we have all the pieces. But it is only when we separate the facts from the fiction that more pieces of the puzzle will be recognized.

You have arrived at Cairo on the east side of the Nile River, and have crossed the Nile to its west bank where the masonry pyramids are spread, within 50 miles (80 km) of each other.

Throughout our imaginary trip, we will be focusing mostly on the pyramids. Therefore, several important but unrelated subjects will not be discussed in this book, such as the Sphinx, temples, tombs, ...etc.

To cover these subjects, we recommend that you check

other publications by Tehuti Research Foundation < http://
www.egypt-tehuti.org >.

Before we check the sites and interiors of the pyramids,
we should review the different views on this very interesting

Partial Map of Egypt

The Fictional Tombs

We were taught in schools that the pyramids are nothing but tombs, which were built by tyrant Pharaohs, and that slaves were used to haul these big stones up temporary ramps, in the construction of these pyramids. True or false?

When we examine the facts at the pyramids, you will find that all these commonly held beliefs about the pyramids are so incredibly illogical that your faith in your education and background may be shattered.

Were the pyramids tombs?

The answer is a resounding *NO*. There is, however, an unusual situation in the case of Zoser's Pyramid at Saqqara. As we will find later in Saqqara, Zoser built complete underground burial chambers for himself and his family. Building a step pyramid on top was an afterthought, constructed a few years later. The burial chambers are not an integral part of the pyramid structure. The nine remaining pyramids, which have been constructed from solid core masonry, are not tombs.

Where did Egyptians bury their kings at that time?

The tombs consisted of subterranean burial chambers with large, low, rectangular, mud-brick superstructures. These types of tombs were called *mastabas*, meaning *benches*.

Typical Offering Scenes in Egyptian Tombs.
The nine pyramids are void of such
scenes or any inscriptions whatsoever.

▲ The subterranean parts contained the burial chambers, which were surrounded by many other chambers and store rooms, for the less important funerary goods. The burial chamber was a narrow chamber hewn out of the rock, to which a shaft leads down from the roof of the mastaba.

▲ The superstructures were rectangular, low in proportion to their lengths, and with convex roofs. They varied in size from 24 sq. yds. (20 sq. m) to an area of more than ¼ acre.

How did they bury their kings at that time?

The kings were buried in simple rectangular wooden chests, covered with funerary texts and inscriptions. The wooden coffin was placed inside a stone sarcophagus, which was also covered with funerary texts and inscriptions.

The viscera (stomach, intestines, lungs, and liver) of the deceased were placed in four individual containers, called *canopic jars*, next to the sarcophagus.

How did the pyramids vary from the normal royal tombs of that time?

The nine solid masonry pyramids, after Zoser's, contain a total of fourteen uninscribed rooms and just three empty, uninscribed stone chests, incorrectly referred to as *sarcophagi*.

The following are the major differences between the pyramids and Egyptian tombs:

▲   *Firstly*, these nine pyramids are totally void of ANY official inscriptions, offering rooms, and other funerary features, found in both earlier and later tombs. The lack of these items, alone, invalidate its function as a tomb, because funerary rites were essential for the deceased's journey in the beyond.

The sacred inscriptions acted as reference guides or maps

A Typical Ancient Mastaba-Type Tomb

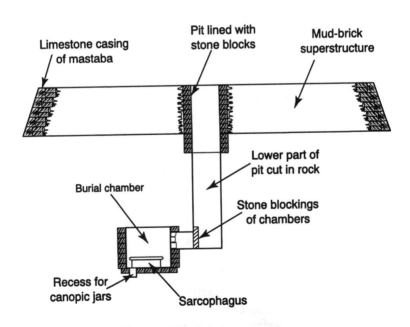

A Cross-Section of a Typical Mastaba-Type Tomb

for the individual to find her/his way through the afterworld, the symbolic and representative figures and sculptures and implements intended to meet whatever needs the individual had in the afterlife.

▲   **Secondly**, there are too few empty "stone chests" and too many empty rooms in these nine pyramids, to theorize that they were tombs.

▲   **Thirdly**, if we accept, hypothetically, that robbers might have smashed the stone chests and their lids, one can hardly accept the logic that these robbers would have taken the trouble to steal the smashed stone chests.
In spite of careful search, no chips of broken stone chests or their lids were found anywhere in the pyramids' passages and chambers.

▲   **Fourthly**, the passageways in the nine pyramids are too narrow to provide for the manipulation of the stone chests. These nine pyramids are clearly lacking adequate space arrangements for people and for manipulating ceremonial objects.
We know from examinations of numerous mummies, from the Pyramid Age Era, that people were taller than five feet (1.5m), which makes these passages [less than 4 feet (1.2m) high] impossible to walk upright.

▲   **Fifthly**, one Pharaoh, Snefru (2575-2551 BCE), built three pyramids, and nobody expects him to be buried in all three of them.

▲   **Lastly**, no human remains were ever found inside the nine masonry pyramids. Thieves steal treasures, but they would naturally avoid dead bodies.

As you review the sites and interiors of these pyramids, you will discover the overwhelming evidence that the pyramids were not built to entomb anybody.

The Genuine Masonry Pyramids

You mentioned ten pyramids, and I thought that there were many more.

There are numerous structures which have/had the shape of a pyramid. The genuine pyramids, however, are those which consist of *solid core masonry*. People forget that a pyramid by geometric definition, as they studied in school, is "a solid figure having a polygonal base, the sides of which form the bases of triangular surfaces meeting at a common vertex".

So, tell me about these genuine masonry pyramids.

These ten pyramids are located within 50 miles (80km) of each other. They were all built during the 3rd and 4th Dynasties. In a little more than a century, 25 million tons of limestone was used to build these pyramids. Later, ungenuine "pyramids" were built during the 5th and later Dynasties.

What are these ungenuine "pyramids" made of?

They are built of loose stone rubble and sand, sandwiched between stone walls. Most are now little more than heaps of rubble, because this type of construction rapidly deteriorates, once the casing is badly damaged or removed.

How about the pyramids of Mexico and China?

These are not pyramids, because they don't have the geometric shape of pyramids. They are basically terraced buildings totally different in shape and function than the ancient Egyptian pyramids.

Okay, so what are the ten masonry pyramids?

They are, in the order that they were built:

3rd Dynasty

	Pharaoh	Reign (BCE)	Location	Notes
1	Zoser	2630-2611	Saqqara	Step Pyramid
2	Sekhemket	2611-2603	Saqqara	Step Pyramid
3	Kha-ba	2603-2599	Z. el Aryan	Layer Pyramid
	Huni	2599-2575	--	?

4th Dynasty

	Pharaoh	Reign (BCE)	Location	Notes
4	Snefru	2575-2551	Meidum	--
5	Snefru	"　　"	Dahshur	Bent Pyramid
6	Snefru	"　　"	Dahshur	Red Pyramid
7	Khufu	2551-2528	Giza	(Cheops)
8	Gedefra	2528-2520	Abu-Rawash	Unfinished
9	Khafra	2520-2494	Giza	(Chephren)
10	Menkaura	2494-2472	Giza	(Mycerinus)

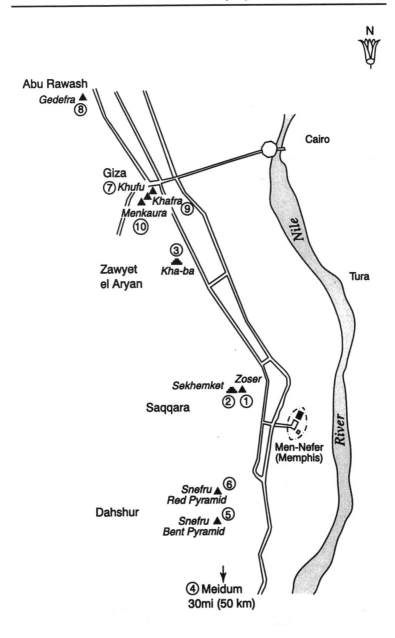

N

Abu Rawash
Gedefra ▲
⑧

Cairo

Giza
⑦ *Khufu* ▲
▲ *Khafra*
Menkaura ⑨
⑩

Nile

Zawyet
el Aryan

③
⊞
Kha-ba

Tura

Sekhemket *Zoser*
⊞ ▲
② ①

Saqqara

Men-Nefer
(Memphis)

River

Snefru ▲ ⑥
Red Pyramid

Dahshur

Snefru ▲ ⑤
Bent Pyramid

↓
④ Meidum
30mi (50 km)

Map of the Ten Pyramids
Numbered in Their Chronological Order

The Pyramid Age started with Pharaoh Zoser, who left his identification in the underground chambers, and later built the Step Pyramid on top.

However, the other nine pyramids are totally void of ANY official inscription. They have been attributed to specific Pharaohs, based on Herodotus' accounts and references that indirectly refer to these Pharaohs' names, on some nearby buildings and tombs.

One should conclude that they were unselfish kings, who built them for a higher and nobler cause, and not as personal monuments.

But why only ten masonry pyramids? Why not more or less?

There was definitely a master plan that required this particular number of pyramids, with their specific size and configuration, and at specific locations.

While we don't know all the answers, that should not give people a license to go wild with unsubstantiated theories.

What do you think then?

We have to understand the totality of the ancient Egyptian thinking, so as to find the answers in the Egyptian context.

I don't believe that it is a coincidence that the Zoser Pyramid is at the center of the other nine (unmarked) pyramids.

Does the number of pyramids (nine) have special significance?

Nine is the number of **neteru** (gods) that took part in the creation process of the universe. These nine **neteru** (meaning cosmic forces) formed the Ennead. Ancient Egyptian texts refer to the Ennead (group of nine) as a single divine entity.

Pyramid Texts

If the pyramids were not tombs, why are these ancient Egyptian funerary texts called "Pyramid Texts"?

This is a deceitful title, which is given by academia, in order to shove it down our throats that the pyramids were tombs.

To untangle their web of deception, we must differentiate between the masonry pyramids and the tombs that are covered by heaps of rubble. Such tombs included these funerary texts.

What are these Funerary "Pyramid" Texts?

They are a collection of funerary literature that was found in the tombs of the Kings of the 5th and 6th Dynasties (2465-2150 BCE).

But weren't the masonry pyramids built earlier, during the 3rd and 4th Dynasties?

Exactly. There are no records of this form of Text prior to the 5th Dynasty, and they don't exist in any of the ten masonry pyramids, which were built between 2630-2472 BCE.

How important were these Texts in ancient Egyptian history?

These Texts form the basis for all subsequent funerary literature in Egypt, such as: *The Book of the Coming Forth by Day* (known mistakenly as *The Book of the Dead*), *The Book of What is in the Duat* (or *Underworld*), *The Book of the Gates*, *The Book of Caverns*, *The Litany of Ra*, *The Book of Aker*, *The Book of Day*, and *The Book of Night*.

Where can we see such Texts?

The most accessible place is in Saqqara, where at the end of the 5th Dynasty, King Unas (2356-2323 BCE) built this small and ungenuine "pyramid", which consists of a heap of rubble, built up to support the outer layers of the core, which in turn, supported the casing stones.

The Funerary *"Pyramid"* Texts are carved on the walls, in the underground burial chamber and its ancillary rooms.

Were the Texts used in Kings' tombs only?

No, they were not only for Kings, but the Texts were also inscribed in the coffins of the nobles.

Do you mean only for rich people?

Not at all. The ancient Egyptian Kings and nobles never lived in stone palaces. They dwelt in mud-brick homes, just like any peasant.

Kings and nobles signify high spiritual attainment, and not social status. By serving (not ruling) their people, they have achieved spiritual purity that will not require them to reincarnate again.

The Funerary Texts help their souls to transform from

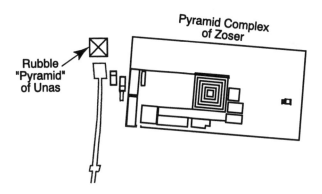

Saqqara Site Plan (Partial)

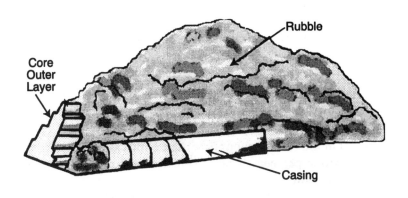

The Rubble "Pyramid" Of Unas

their earthly existence to, as the ancient Egyptian writings describe it,

become a star of gold and join the company of Ra, and sail with him in his boat of millions of years.

So, these Texts formed the ancient Egyptian canon?

No, not at all. They were not a singular rigid canon. The texts varied somewhat from one tomb to another. The texts reflect various interpretations in the different tombs.

There was never a single religious authority who had the power or the desire to choose some writings and incorporate them into one canon, except during Akhenaton's reign (1367-1361 BCE), which was an aberration.

How about Akhenaton?

This is a major subject that you will find covered thoroughly in Tehuti Research Foundation's other publications.

So, we can learn a lot about the ancient Egyptians from these Texts?

Only if we have an open mind. Unfortunately, we have three major problems:

1) The status of our understanding of ancient Egyptian language is very weak and is based on numerous assumptions that are themselves error-prone. The number of the "translated" ancient Egyptian words are less than 1% of the number of words in an average English language dictionary.

2) The Western academic Egyptologists and their Egyptian

academic followers look at the ancient Egyptian Texts through their Judeao-Christian-Moslem paradigms. They are extremely narrow-minded and as usual, very arrogant.

3.   In addition to the dire status of decipherment of the ancient Egyptian language, there is another major concern that is neglected by the Western academia, which is the need to understand the peculiar symbolism in the ancient Egyptian texts and works.

Is it really that bad?

As it stands, the present translations of these Funerary Texts are tenuous in the extreme. There are at least five major versions that exist in various European languages. They differ radically when they deal with the prayers and spiritual instructions, based on the attitude of the translator/interpreter.

When academicians espouse the view that they are dealing with the works of superstitious primitives, the translations will reflect that conviction.

Can you give me an example?

R.O. Faulkner's translation of "Utterance 316" of the Funerary Texts: (the question marks are the translator's):

The phallus of Babi is drawn back, the doors of the sky are opened, the King has opened [the doors of the sky] because of the furnace heat which the gods pour out. What Heru lets slip (?) the King lets slip (?) there into this furnace heat which the gods pour out. They make a road for the King that the King may pass on it, for the King is Heru.

This does not make any sense whatsoever.

These big-name academicians, rather than recognizing that they don't understand the ancient Egyptian language and culture, they shamelessly blame the ancient Egyptians for their own shortcomings.

It is unwise to label the ancient writing as confusing or superstitious. Their symbolism then is as unique as our symbolism now.

A symbol is something that represents something else by association or resemblance. Most, if not all, symbols have private meaning known only to a group of people at a certain time in history. Symbols need only represent something meaningful to a particular intended audience.

If we don't understand their symbolism, it is not because they are being secretive. Likewise, symbols in our own countries were not created to keep any secrets. Symbolism is present in everything we do in life. It is subtle like breathing — we are unaware of it most of the time.

Δ   Δ   Δ

Pyramid Construction Techniques

The Common Theory

What is the 'common' theory about how the pyramid was built?

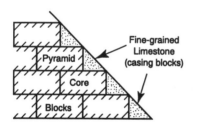

To begin with, we should mention that the 'common' theory has no historical evidence to support it. Many academic Egyptologists claim that there are no ancient Egyptian records from any period, which describe how the pyramids were built. Their error is that they have pre-determined the construction method, and are only seeking the records to affirm their pre-conceived theory.

Their '*invented*' theory is that:

1. The pyramid's core was built mostly of quarried local limestone blocks which were cemented by a paper thin layer of mortar.

2. The core masonry was originally faced with fine-grained limestone, which was quarried from Tura on the east bank of the Nile and ferried across the Nile to the site.

What did Herodotus say about that?

Herodotus neither mentioned the source of the core masonry as local limestone nor that the pyramid blocks were carved. He stated that stones (not necessarily quarried blocks, but possibly stone rubble) were brought to the site from the east side of the Nile.

Here is an excerpt from Herodotus' account:

*"This pyramid was built thus; in the form of steps, which some call crosae, and others call bomides. After preparing the foundation, they raised stones by using **machines** made of short planks of wood, which raised the stones from the ground to the first range of steps. On this range there was another **machine** which received the stone upon arrival. Another **machine** advanced the stone on the second step. Either there were as many **machines** as steps, or there was really only one, and portable, to reach each range in succession whenever they wished to raise the stone higher. I am telling both possibilities because both were mentioned."*

I am confused about Herodotus' statement that *"they raised stones by using machines made of short planks of wood."*

The Greek word, *mechane*, used by Herodotus, is a non-specific generic term indicating a type of device.

A machine that is made of short planks of wood does not make much sense.

Many people ridiculed Herodotus for his description. It was actually the poor translation that caused the confusion. The translators distorted the meaning of the Greek word, when they gave it a specific modern-day meaning.

When the word, *mechane*, is translated to mean a device such as *mold*, the whole description makes sense. Let us review it in such a form:

"... They raised stones by using **molds** *made of short planks of wood, which raised the stones from the ground to the first range of steps. On this range there was another* **mold** *which received the stone [rubble] upon arrival. Another* **mold** *advanced the stone on the second step. Either there were as many* **molds** *as steps, or there was really only one, and portable, to reach each range in succession whenever they wished to raise the stone higher. I am telling both possibilities because both were mentioned."*

A mold can be considered as an apparatus or device. If Herodotus was not familiar with the term '*mold*', he therefore used the more general term, '*mechane*'.

What were the wooden plank molds used for?

They were used to hold the man-made concrete in block-shaped form, until the concrete dried.

Δ   Δ   Δ

Egyptian Know-How

What is the evidence that shows the ancient Egyptians had the know-how to make such stones?

The most overwhelming evidence was found in Saqqara, in some rooms underneath the Zoser Pyramid, which yielded about 40,000 items of stone jars and vessels, of every imaginable size, shape, and material, many of which were damaged due to settling of the earth. Most of these manufactured vessels were produced in earlier eras. The items are made of slate, metamorphic schist (stone containing layers of flaky minerals,) diorite, and basalt. The diorite used, a granite rock, is among the hardest known. Modern sculptors do not attempt to carve these varieties of stone.

Numerous hard stone vessels were found with long, narrow necks, and wide rounded bellies. Their interiors and exteriors correspond perfectly. These smooth and glossy vessels show no traces of tool marks.

How were all these small and large items made from such hard stones? And moreover, how could such hard stones be worked with no trace of tool marks?

They did not use tools because there are no tool marks. Their advanced knowledge in alchemy (the word chemistry was derived from it only 250 years ago) enabled them to do wonders in chemical and metallurgical applications. Many of these items could have been manufactured from mineral ores and then molded, rather than sculpted or engraved.

One of the titles of the famed Imhotep was *Maker of Vases in Chief.*

Different types of vessels had different functions, in all aspects of the ancient (and modern rural) Egyptians' lives.

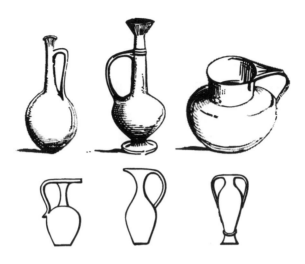

Samples of Found Vessels

A bas-relief showing the hollowing out of Egyptian alabaster vase by a liquid in a skin or bladder

So, these 40,000 items were not manufactured during Zoser's reign?

No. They were crafted in previous eras and collected and stored by him in these chambers underneath his pyramid.

Why did Zoser do that, to claim that they were his?

Zoser never claimed that. He must have collected them to put them in a safe place.

How far back were these vessels made?

Much earlier than what academic Egyptologists want to admit.

But ancient Egyptian dynastic history started by Mena (Menes), ca. 3050 BCE, just 4 centuries before Zoser.

Ancient Egyptian history is much older than the dynastic history, based on the following facts:

1. Temples throughout Egypt make reference to being originally built much earlier than its dynastic history.

2. The 40,000 items found underneath the 3rd Dynasty pyramid of Zoser are indicative of much earlier knowledge and civilization.

3. The Funerary (Pyramid) Texts in Unas' Tomb in Saqqara contain repeated references to a prior inauguration of the New Year (when the civil calendar year of 365 days and the Sothic calendar year coincide every 1460 of such years). Astronomical calculations show that the referenced prior New Year occurred in 4240 BCE. We don't

know if this was the first time that Egyptians calculated the time of the New Year, or if other prior New Years occurred in previous Sothic periods. If 4240 BCE was the first recorded New Year, the observation and calculation of the differences between the solar and sothic cycles must have started at a very remote age.

4.   The Greek and Roman writers of antiquity, basing their accounts on information received either first or second-hand from Egyptian sources, claimed a far greater antiquity for the Egyptian civilization than that currently established by academicians. These Egyptian sources called for antiquity ranging from 24,000 and 36,000 years during which Egypt was civilized.

5.   Herodotus reported that he was informed by Egyptian priests that the sun had twice set where it now rose, and twice risen where it now set. Egyptologist Schwaller de Lubicz explained the statement to mean that it may be a reference to the progressional cycles of the equinox. The progression results in the rising against a different sign of the Zodiac approximately every two thousand years. This would mean that the Egyptians counted their history back for at least a cycle and a half, some 36,000 years. This is in a general agreement with other accounts and evidential findings.

6.   The remote age of the Sphinx of Giza, and the **Ausarion** (Oserion) at **Abtu** (Abydos), ...etc.

So why do history books state that ancient Egyptian civilization started with **Mena** (ca. 3050 BCE), if it is so much older?

The Greco-Egyptian historian Manetho (3rd century BCE), under the early Ptolemies, wrote the only substantive history of Egypt to come down to us. He gathered his information from Egyptian records. A few pre-dynastic inscribed tablets

and papyri have been found, but all were incomplete because
of their remote age. <u>Manetho acknowledged greater antiquity
of the Egyptian history</u>. However, because of the overwhelming task, he chose **Mena**(Menes) as a starting point, about 3,000
years earlier.

•   •   •

Back to our original point, are you saying that the ancient Egyptians manufactured hard stones from mineral ores?

Yes. Their knowledge in manufacturing stones was also
utilized to manufacture the blocks for the masonry pyramids.

What is your evidence to support the idea of man-made stone blocks?

There are references to making stones on a stele, commonly known as the *"Famine Stele,"* located on the island of
Sehel, near Elephantine, south of **Sunt** (Aswan). The stele is
dated to about 200 BCE. It is a copy of an Old Kingdom text,
which dates to the reign of
Zoser, 2500 years earlier.

The three main charac-
ters on the stele, are Khnum
(who represents the Divine
Principle of Molding), King
Zoser, and Imhotep.

This stele should have
been named *Khnum's Al-
chemical Stele*, for it holds
the key to the method of
manufacturing man-made
stone.

Approximately one-
third of this stele's content

Khnum, The Divine Molder,
at the potter's wheel

pertains to rocks and mineral ore, and their processing.

Columns 18 and 19 of this Stele quote the Divine Molder, Khnum, speaking to King Zoser:

"I am Khnum, your creator, ... I give you rare ore after rare ore....Never before has anyone processed them (to make stone) in order to build the monuments ....".

Very interesting. Tell me more.

Let us review how the ancient and even some modern Egyptians make bricks. They push wet Nile mud, mixed with straw and sand, into a wooden mold. Then the soft bricks are set out to dry in the hot sun.

Therefore, using wooden molds to shape the limestone concrete materials into large blocks was nothing new to them.

I never thought about it this way.

To show their extensive knowledge, let us remember that the ancient Egyptians had the skills in complicated processes to imitate the rich brilliance of natural and precious stones. Some of their mock pearls were so well counterfeited, that even now it is difficult to differentiate them from real pearls, even with a strong lens.

Pliny the Elder (23-79 CE), the Roman naturalist, stated in *The Encyclopedia of Natural History*, Book 31, that Egyptians made real rocks from a multitude of minerals. He also stated that Egyptians made vases from their man-made stone.

So, making stones to build the pyramid should not have been a major achievement for them.

Of course not. They had been manufacturing many other stones for a long time. Making stone blocks for the pyramid was just another application of their knowledge at that time.

The Source of the Stones

But are you saying that these stones could NOT have been quarried, as we were told?

As we stated earlier, the 'common' story is that the blocks, for the pyramids, were quarried from local sources, and that the casing blocks came from Tura, across the River Nile.

Furthermore, the 'common' story claims that the ancient Egyptians used the following, to cut and shape the stone blocks:

1- copper chisels and possibly iron tools
2- flint, quartz and diorite pounders
3- large wooden crow bars

The 'common' story also claims that to transport the stone blocks, they used wooden sledges and rollers.

What is wrong with this theory?

Firstly, because the 'common' theory is only a guess, and there is no historical evidence to support it.

Secondly, stone and copper tools would not have been able to produce these huge numbers of blocks, with such a high quality, in the allocated construction time period, for each of the pyramids.

Could it have been that they used a different method to quarry stones?

To quarry stones, some suggested that the Egyptians may have heated the surface of the stone to a very high temperature with fire, then sprayed on water to make it split. This suggestion is invalid, because:

Firstly, this method results in providing irregular surfaces and not in making regular-shaped blocks.

This method can only be used to reduce large pieces of sandstone, granite, or basalt into small, irregular, fragmented aggregates.

Secondly, heating with fire transfers limestone into lime at 704° (1,300°F). As such, producing pyramid blocks by heating limestone, is impossible.

So how did they do it?

I believe that these blocks were high quality man-made limestone concrete and not quarried natural stone.

It is a known fact that the ancient Egyptian silico-aluminate cement mortar is far superior to present day hydrated calcium sulfate mortar. By mixing the ancient high quality cement with fossil-shell limestone, the Egyptians were able to produce high quality limestone concrete.

The synthetic blocks consist basically of about 90-95% limestone rubble, and 5-10% cement.

All the required ingredients to make synthetic concrete stone, with no appreciable shrinkage, are plentiful in Egypt:

1 - The *alumina*, used for low temperature mineral synthesis, is contained in the mud from the Nile River.

2 - *Natron salt* (sodium carbonate) is very plentiful in the Egyptian deserts and salt lakes.

3 - *Lime*, which is the most basic ingredient for cement production, was easily obtained by calcining limestone in simple hearths.

4 - The Sinai mines contained *arsenic minerals,* needed to produce rapid hydraulic setting, for large concrete blocks.

Natron (a type of flux) reacts with lime and water to produce caustic soda (sodium hydroxide), which is the main ingredient for alchemically making stone.

Are there any records about the source of the arsenic minerals, used to manufacture the stone?

Records of mining activities during Zoser's reign are indicated on a stele at the mines of Wadi Maghara in Sinai. Similar mining activities, during the subsequent Pharaohs' reigns of the 3rd and 4th Dynasties, are also recorded at Sinai.

Δ   Δ   Δ

Synthetic and Natural Blocks

To add to the evidence that the blocks were are not natural stone but are high quality limestone concrete (synthetic stone) which was cast directly in place, let us consider the following undisputed facts about the **Khufu** (Cheops) Pyramid of Giza. [Similar facts to those mentioned here are also applicable to all masonry pyramids.]

1. The Great Pyramid contains approximately 2.6 million building blocks, weighing from two to seventy tons apiece.

2. Almost none of the pyramid blocks match the Giza bedrock chemically or mineralogically.

3. The bedrock of the Giza Palteau is made of strata, while the pyramid blocks contain no strata.

4. Strata and defects make it impossible to cut stone to perfectly uniform dimensions.

5. Geologists and geochemists cannot agree on the origin of the pyramid blocks. This alone shatters the common theory that the core masonry of the pyramid was quarried from local bedrock.

6. Natural stone consists of fossil shells which lie horizontally or flat in the bedrock, as a result of forming sedimentary layers of bedrock, over millions of years.

Drawing from *Description de l'Egypte*, written between 1809 and 1813 by Francois Jomard, shows jumbled shells in pyramid core blocks.

The blocks of the masonry pyramids of Egypt show jumbled shells which is indicative of man-made cast stone. In any concrete, the aggregate are jumbled, and as a result, cast concrete is devoid of sedimentary layers.

These pyramids consisted essentially of fossil shell limestone, a heterogeneous material very difficult to cut precisely.

7. There are about ten standard block lengths throughout the pyramid. Similarly, limited numbers of standard sizes apply in other pyramids as well.
Carving such highly uniform dimensions is impossible. However, having standardized concrete forming molds is a more logical conclusion.

8. It was found that the longest blocks in the pyramids always have the same length. This is extremely strong evidence in favor of the use of casting molds.

9. The French scientists found that the bulk density of the pyramid blocks is 20 % lighter than the local bedrock limestone. Cast blocks are always 20-25 % lighter than natural rock, because they are full of air bubbles.

10. Copper tools (which are a soft metal), used by Egyptians at that time, cannot cut large granite or millions of limestone blocks, within the timespan of the builders of the masonry pyramids.

11. Limestone frequently splits during cutting. Faults and strata in bedrock assure that for every block cut to standard, at least one will crack or be improperly sized during quarrying.

Given the many millions of blocks of all these pyramids, there should be millions of cracked blocks lying nearby or somewhere in Egypt, but they are nowhere to be found. In short, no rubbish of cracked blocks means no quarrying. Ancient historians, who documented their visits to Egypt, have not mentioned heaps of broken blocks.

This is too much evidence.

You now know the hard facts. Based on the elements of the "common theory" of stone cutting, hauling, and hoisting, how can we logically answer the following questions:

1. Where did they get the huge quantity required to build this and other pyramids from? There is no physical evidence of such a source, whatsoever.

2. How did they manage to make the sloping sides of the pyramids absolutely flat?

3. How did they make the four sloping sides meet at a perfect point at the summit?

4. How did they make the tiers so level?

5. How did they cut the stones, so that they fit together so precisely?

6. What tools did they use?

7. How could the required number of workers (estimated at 240-300,000 people) maneuver on the confined building site?

8. How did they cut the blocks so uniform?

9. How did they place some of the heaviest blocks in the pyramid, at such great heights?

10. How were 115,000 casing blocks all made to fit to a hair's breadth and closer, as was the case in Khufu's pyramid?

11. How was all the work done in about 20 years?

All these questions invalidate the "common theory". Common sense, along with the physical evidence, lead to the conclusion that the blocks were man-made.

The idea of molding the pyramid blocks is intriguing.

Let me help you with other information.

In 1974, a team from Stanford Research Institute (SRI) of Stanford University, used electromagnetic sounding equipment to locate hidden rooms. The waves, sent out, were absorbed by the high moisture content of the blocks. As a result, the mission failed.

How can the pyramid attract moisture in the midst of an arid desert area?

Only concrete blocks retain moisture, which is further evidence showing that the pyramid blocks were synthetic and not quarried.

Okay. Do you have more evidence?

Let us take a closer look at some of these blocks.

1. The paper-thin mortar between the stone blocks does not provide any cohesive power between the stone blocks. This paper-thin mortar is actually the result of excess water in the concrete slurry. The weight of aggregates in the concrete mix squeezes watery cement to the surface, where it sets, to form the thin surface mortar layer.

2. Organic fibers, air bubbles, and an artificial red coating are visible on some blocks. All are indicative of the casting process of man-made, and not natural stone.

3. The top layers of several blocks are quite riddled with holes. The deteriorated layers look like sponges. The denser bottom layer didn't deteriorate.
    In a concrete mix, air bubbles and excess watery binder

rise to the top, producing a lighter, weaker form.
The rough top layer is always about the same size, regardless of the height of the block.

This phenomena is evident at all the pyramids and temples of Giza, i.e. light weight, weathered and weak top portions, which is indicative of cast concrete, and not natural stone.

4.   The largest blocks, found throughout the ancient Egyptian monuments of Giza, exhibit many wavy lines and not horizontal lines. Wavy lines occur when concrete casting is stopped for several hours (such as an overnight stoppage). The earlier casted concrete consolidates, and the result is a wavy line that develops between it and the next concrete pour/cast.

Strata in the bedrock are horizontal and straight, while wavy lines result when material is poured into a mold. (Also refer to page 152.)

5.   Modern mortar consists exclusively of hydrated calcium sulfate.
Ancient Egyptian mortar is based on a silico-aluminate, a result of geopolymerization.

6.   The only surviving record of the activities of Khnum-Khufu's reign are scenes engraved in Sinai, indicating extensive mining expeditions of arsenic minerals required for making stones.

Δ   Δ   Δ

The Casing Stones

How about the casing stones?

Δ   The core masonry of the pyramids were dressed with casing blocks, made of fine-grained limestone that appears to be polished, and which would have shone brilliantly in the Egyptian sun.

Δ   The four sloping faces of the **Khufu** Pyramid were originally dressed with 115,000 of these casing stones — 5.5 acres of them on each of its four faces. Each weighed ten to fifteen tons apiece. The Greek historian, Herodotus, stated that the joints between them were so finely dressed, as to be nearly invisible. A tolerance of .01 inch was the maximum found between these stones — so tight that a paper cannot fit between them.

Were the surfaces of the casing stones totally blank?

No. Herodotus and others referred to the inscriptions, which were said to cover the outside of some pyramids.

Even in the days of the Arab Period, the traveler Abd el Latif (b. 1179 CE) mentioned that the inscriptions on **Khufu**'s pyramid, if copied, would fill 10,000 pages.

What happened to the casing stones and the inscribed documents on their surfaces?

Casing stones were quarried during and after the 13th century, to build mosques and palaces, or for burning lime.

Perfect fit between the casing stones

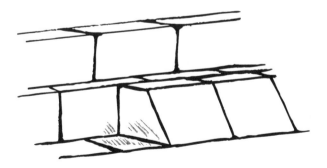

Remainder of some casing stones at Khufu's Pyramid

How were the casing blocks molded?

The casing blocks, in the 4th Dynasty pyramids, were angled to produce the slope of the pyramid. Because of their shape, the casing blocks were cast in an inverted position against neighboring blocks. Once they hardened, the concrete forms were removed and the blocks were then turned upside down and positioned.

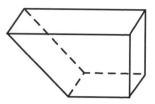

Inverted position of a casing block, as it was cast.

Any evidence to such practice?

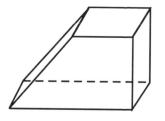

Final position of a casing block.

Yes. Researchers found that the inscriptions on the casing stones of the Red Pyramid of Snefru and the **Khufu** Pyramid are always on the bottom of the casing blocks. This is good evidence that they were cast in the inverted position. Had the casing blocks been carved, inscriptions would be found on various sides, and not just one position.

Δ   Δ   Δ

The Fictional Ramps

How about these temporary ramps, which the Egyptians used to build the pyramids?

Δ   This is a total invention, but it has been repeated so many times that it became a fact, in most peoples' minds.

Δ   Herodotus never mentioned such ramps. His historical account described the typical stone causeway between the base of the pyramid and the Valley Temple. This causeway was a permanent feature which was, as Herodotus described, 3300' (1006m) long, 60' (18m) wide and 48' (15m) high, and not used to haul blocks.

Δ   Many academicians want to believe that the only way to build the pyramid is by increasing both the height and length of a temporary ramp, as it was raised to the successive levels of the pyramid.

Was it at least possible?

No.

Δ   The people who are stuck on the ramps theory, make reference to what appears to be a mud ramp, found at Sekhemket's Pyramid in Saqqara. Even if it was a ramp, it was only 23' (7m) high. The constructed pyramids are much higher than that.

Δ   The Danish civil engineer, P. Garde-Hanson, calculated that to build a ramp all the way to the top of the Khufu Pyramid would require 17.5 million cubic yards of material (seven times the amount needed for the pyramid itself). A work force of 240,000 would have been needed to build such a ramp, within Khufu's reign of 23 years.

Δ   To dismantle the ramp at the completion of **Khufu**'s pyramid, it would have required a work force of 300,000 and a further eight years. Such a huge amount of rubbish is not visible anywhere in the vicinity and was never mentioned by earlier historians.

Δ   After reaching such unbelievable figures, Garde-Hanson theorized a combination of a ramp and a lifting device. He theorized a ramp that would reach halfway up the pyramid. At such a level, about 90 percent of the material needed for the pyramid would have been used. The second element of his modified theory, i.e. the mysterious lifting device of some kind, was and still is an unresolved question.

Hypothetically, let's we agree with Garde-Hanson's theories, and try to visualize the staggering figures: 4,000 year-round quarrymen producing 330 blocks per day. During inundation season, 4,000 blocks per day are transported to the Nile, ferried across, hauled up the ramp to the Giza plateau, and set into place in the core — at a rate of 6.67 blocks per minute! Imagine 6.67 blocks every 60 seconds! This rate is impossible to achieve. This is another reason to disregard the validity of the quarrying and ramp theories.

Δ   What is even more staggering is the case of Snefru (**Khufu**'s predecessor). It means that Snefru, in the course of his reign of 24 years, was responsible for the production, transport, and dressing of **several times the quantity of the Great Pyramid**. Even trying to calculate the logistics of such work, in modern terms, is too overwhelming.

Δ   Building and removing such ramps would have been a much greater task than building this or other pyramids alone. Therefore, as academicians dream up "primitive means" for ancient Egyptians, they complicate their own unfounded theories.

Δ   Δ   Δ

Abandonment Problems

Are the interiors of the solid masonry pyramids the same as the non-masonry heaps of rubble?

As stated earlier, the genuine solid stone pyramids have narrow passageways and some empty rooms, which are totally void of any funerary inscriptions and features.

On the other hand, the later ungenuine heaps of rubble have spacious passageways, and burial and offering rooms that are covered with funerary texts.

I read that ancient Egyptians changed their mind during the building of the pyramids, and had to abandon earlier work.

The *abandonment theory* is the common escape route for those people who made up their minds before considering all the evidence. Once they adopted the idea that the pyramids were tombs, they had to twist the evidence to fit into their stubborn theories. In the process, they had no problem fabricating answers.

In the Giza and Dahshur pyramids, which provide no evidence of any kind of burials at all, almost every pyramid, according to this crazy theory, underwent one or several of these peculiar *changes of mind*. Even odder is the fact that the Giza and Dahshur pyramids are more superior than the pyramids that followed — in every respect of size, workmanship, and elaboration.

Yes. It is peculiar that we hear of this abandonment theory only at the best pyramids.

Δ It is worth mentioning that in none of the later ungenuine
   pyramids used for burials, have the same abandonists
   claimed that ANY changes of plan took place.

Δ The precision and perfection of everything you see in the
   Giza and Dahshur Pyramids, shows thorough, well-
   thought-out pre-planning.

Δ Just because we don't know the purpose of everything we
   see, that does not give us a license to fabricate answers
   and corrupt history.

   Later, when we investigate the interiors of these pyramids,
we will discuss the so-called abandoned rooms and changed
plans. The evidence is contrary to academia's wild and unfounded notions.

Δ   Δ   Δ

Pyramid Power

You talked earlier about the significance of nine, as the number of pyramids. The question is, what is the purpose of these pyramids?

There is no direct evidence that we know of, at this time, to answer this question. However, once we grasp the main function of the ancient Egyptian stone buildings, we can easily see their connection to the supernatural forces of the universe. Ancient Egyptian monuments, such as the pyramids and other temples, were deliberately constructed at specific sites with specific orientations.

But are there differences between the stone pyramids and the temples?

Yes, the pyramids were closed and sealed structures. They were not open for daily activities/rituals, which was the case in the Egyptian temples.

As you will see later (pages 93 & 94), each pyramid was a part of a complex that contained some temples. So, all the rituals were carried out in these temples, and not in the pyramids.

The stone pyramids were aligned with the cardinal points, which indicates the significance of earth, in their function. The temples in other regions of Egypt were each positioned according to astronomical alignments, i.e. the earth in relationship to other heavenly bodies.

So, if the sealed stone pyramids were not used for rituals, what could be their function?

The pyramids were harmonically proportioned to act/ function in the same fashion as greenhouses, i.e. to attract and retain certain energies. In the case of the pyramid, it should be called the *bluehouse effect.*

Remind me, what is the greenhouse effect?

It is the retention of heat from sunlight at the earth's surface, caused by atmospheric carbon dioxide that admits shortwave radiation but absorbs the longwave radiation emitted by the earth.

So, the bluehouse effect would work along the same principle?

In the case of the bluehouse effect, the building retains the orgone energy.

What is orgone energy?

Orgone comes from outer space. It is what makes the stars twinkle, and the sky blue.

Orgone can be accumulated by building a box with wood on the outside and sheet iron on the inside. The organic material lets the orgone through, and the metal interior reflects it. This condition/phenomenon could therefore be called the *bluehouse effect.* Abnormally high concentrations of psi-org energy build up inside such a box.

What is psi-org energy?

Psi-org combines abbreviations for psychic and orgone energy. They are different names for the same force. The psi field, which produces the human aura and is responsible for all psychic powers, is none other than what Wilhelm Reich, Freud's controversial Austrian disciple, called orgone energy.

The Egyptians knew all about psi-org energy, because they used it. The ancient Egyptians were the first to discover that the shape of the well-proportioned pyramid can concentrate the psi-org energy.

The *bluehouse effect* increases drastically when the surface of the pyramid is laminated.

But, was the pyramid laminated?

Yes, definitely. Early historians and travelers told us how the casing stones of the pyramids used to shine.

Was ther any testing done on this type of energy?

Dr. Harald Puton, a very competent Belgian physicist, found that every form of psi energy is increased by sitting under such a harmonically-proportioned pyramid. A person is more telepathic, more clairvoyant, more precognitive. It is easier to initiate out-of-body experiences under these conditions. Additionally, the body's aura is more intense inside a pyramid.

Any other supporting physical evidence?

The facts are that if you place highly perishable materials

in the so-called *King's Room* of the Khufu Pyramid, or in a similar model of the pyramid, the materials decompose at a much slower rate than if placed anywhere else in the world.

Also, people who experiment with blunt old-fashioned carbon steel razor blades, by placing them overnight in a model pyramid, they find that the dull blades regain their edges by the next morning.

The evidence from all experiments is clear that the pyramid shape itself is responsible somehow for altering or affecting the physical, chemical and biological processes, that might take place within a well-proportioned pyramid shape.

So, a person may feel this powerful energy inside the pyramid.

One feels the power of these pyramids, when inside or outside them, because their configuration is harmonically proportioned.

Δ   Δ   Δ

Harmonic Proportions

What attracts people worldwide to these pyramids?

People love to look at them. They are overwhelmed by the sheer size and beauty. They are beautiful because they are proportionally harmonious and appealing to our inner as well as outer feelings.

Gustave Flaubert, in *Letters from Egypt, 1840*, sums it up:

"There is something curious about them, these famous pyramids, the more one looks at them, the bigger they become."

The slopes of the pyramids were not arbitrarily determined for their aesthetic appearance, but as a result of particular geometrical criteria, and investigations into ratios between their parts: height, edges, base, and so on.

So, they were aware of what Plato later described as "sacred geometry"?

Geometry is not a good word for it, because geometry means *the measure of the earth*. The subject is better described as *harmonic proportions*, where all figures could be drawn or created using a straight line (not even necessarily a ruler) and compass, i.e. without measurement (dependent on proportion only).

Ancient Egyptians were more than aware of it — they created it and executed it. Harmonic proportions are evident in their temples, buildings, theology, ...etc. The ancient Egyptian design followed these principles in well-detailed canons.

How early did ancient Egyptians implement harmonic proportion (sacred geometry)?

The evidence is clear as far back as the Zoser Complex (2630-2611 BCE), which consists of a double square, i.e. its sides have an exact ratio of 1:2, and align perfectly with the cardinal points.

The most conspicuous element of Egyptian architectural design is the 1:2 rectangle, where it was important in the elements or the general outline of the plan.

The diagonal of a 1:2 rectangle is very significant. In a religious sense, when the one became two, the result (diagonal) is the universe. The diagonal symbolizes the functions of creation itself.

For more information, see the book, *Egyptian Harmony: The Visual Music*, ISBN 0-9652509-8-9.

How did the pyramids conform to divine harmonious proportion?

Later on, as we check the site of each pyramid, we will examine each's harmonic proportion.

What is the key to divine harmonic proportion (sacred geometry)?

The key is the relationship between progression of growth and proportion. Harmonic proportion and progression are the essence of the created universe. It is consistent with nature around us. Nature around us follows this harmonious relationship. The natural progression follows a series that is popularized in the West as the "Fibonacci Series".

What is the "Fibonacci Series"?

It is a summation series. Since it was in existence before Fibonacci (born in 1179 CE), it should not bear his name. Fibonacci himself and his Western commentators, did not even claim that it was his "creation". Let us call it as it is - a Summation Series. It is a progressive series, where you start with a number, say 1, then you add this number to its preceding number, and on and on; any figure is the sum of the two preceding ones. The series would therefore be: 1, 1, 2, 3, 5, 8, 13, 21, 34, 55, 89, 144, 233, 377, 610, . . .

This series is reflected throughout nature. The number of seeds in a sunflower, the petals of any flower, the arrangement of pine cones, the growth of a nautilus shell, etc...all follow the same pattern of these harmonious continuous additions.

Was the Summation Series known to the ancient Egyptians?

Yes, with overwhelming evidence. Many ancient Egyptian plans of temples and tombs, throughout the history of ancient Egypt, show along their longitudinal axis and transversely, dimensions in cubits of 1.72' (0.523 m), giving "in clear" consecutive terms of the Summation Series 3, 5, 8, 13, 21, 34, 55, 89, 144, 233, 377, 610, . . .

The Summation Series conforms perfectly with, and can be regarded as an expression of, Egyptian mathematics, which has been defined by everyone as an essentially additive procedure. The summation character of the series, and its use, would be in accord with the practical aspect of Egyptian science. This additivity is obvious in their reduction of multiplication and division to the same process by breaking up higher multiples into a sum of consecutive duplications.

What is the earliest evidence of such knowledge?

There is evidence about the knowledge of the Summation
Series, ever since the Pyramid (erroneously known as *mortu-*
ary) Temple of **Khafra** (Chephren), at Giza, built in 2500 BCE,
i.e. about 3700 years before Fibonacci.

Notice how the essential points of the temple (on the opposite page) comply with the Summation Series, which reaches
the figure of 233 cubits in its total length, as measured from
the pyramid, with a complete series of TEN numbers of the
series.

Was it just a coincidence that occurred in this temple?

Not at all. The ancient Egyptians designed according to a
very strict canon of proportion. The evidence is overwhelming, of this detailed canon and its application throughout the
history of ancient Egypt. For more information, see the book,
Egyptian Harmony: The Visual Music, ISBN 0-9652509-8-9.

What is the other significance of this Series?

This series was the origin of ancient Egyptian harmonic
design. It offers the true pulsation of natural growth. As an
example, the ratio between each group of two consecutive numbers follows the human heartbeat pulsation: sudden increase,
a small dip, a rise again, and then even progression, until the
next heartbeat. So, as the series progresses, the ratio between
successive numbers tends towards the **Neb** (Golden) Proportion, to which Western academia assigned the Greek alphabet
letter ϕ, even though it was known and used long before the
Greeks. And what is worse is that there is not even factual
evidence that the Greeks knew it at all!

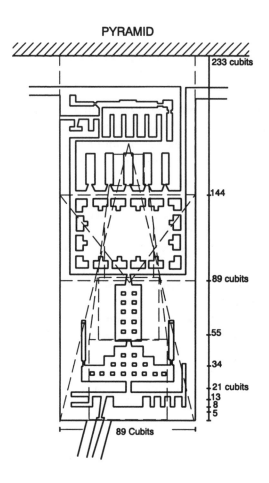

Temple of Khafra (Chephren) at Giza

What is Neb?

Neb is an ancient Egyptian hieroglyphic symbol that is in the shape of a well-proportioned segment of a circle. Neb means *gold*.

Can the Neb (Golden) Proportion be obtained geometrically?

Yes, there are many ways (see *Egyptian Harmony: The Visual Music*). One of these ways is to use a rectangle with sides of 1:2. As stated earlier, ancient Egyptian monuments include plenty of such 1:2 rectangular outlines.

Is there any other evidence to show the ancient Egyptian knowledge of this harmonic proportion?

The 5:8 isosceles triangle, where the height is to the base as 5 is to 8, was by far the most widely used in constructional and harmonic diagrams throughout ancient Egyptian's history. It was no whim for Viollet-le-Duc to call it the *Egyptian Triangle*. The ratio of 8:5 (1.625) represents the most practical ratio of the Summation Series, which is the closest to the theoretical value of the Neb (Golden) Proportion of 1.618.

You can find ancient Egyptian amulets with the 5:8 isosceles triangle, among other geometric shapes, throughout the museums of the world.

Are there other aspects of the ancient Egyptian's knowledge and application of Harmonic Proportion (sacred geometry)?

Oh, yes. But in this book, we will deal with the subject only as it relates to the ten stone pyramids of Egypt.

THE TEN PYRAMIDS

Saqqara

Our first stop is Saqqara where the first two masonry pyramids were built. Saqqara is about an hour's drive from Cairo.

This is a huge area.

Yes, Saqqara was one of two major necropoli of ancient Egypt. The other one was Abtu (*Abydos*).

Can you give an overview of the site?

The origin of the Arabic name, "*Saqqara*", is derived from the name of the Egyptian neter(*god*) Seker *(Sokar)*, who was one of the Men-Nefer(Memphis) Triad: Ptah-Seker-Nefertum.

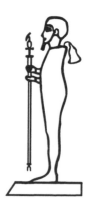

Throughout the history of dynastic Egypt, until the end of the Greek rule under the Ptolemies, Saqqara was the place where every important person left their mark. It is therefore a very important archeological site. Uncovering and discovering important archeological artifacts goes on, and will continue to go on here, for decades to come.

Ptah

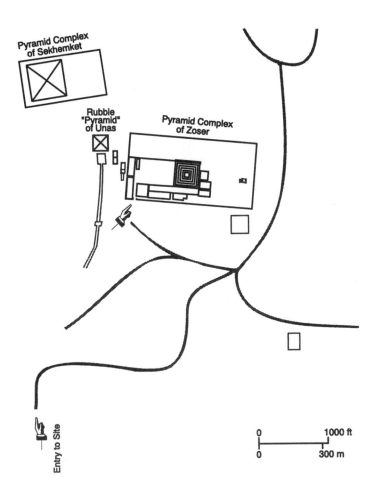

Saqqara Site Plan (Partial)

The Pyramid Complex of Zoser

The Step Pyramid of Zoser is located within the boundaries of the Pyramid Complex of Zoser. This complex was built during the reign of King Zoser (2630-2611 BCE).

The Complex contains, in addition to the Step Pyramid, several buildings, colonnades and temples. The whole Zoser Complex is a masterpiece of harmony and order.

Was this the first time Egyptians used stone in their buildings?

Prior to Zoser, stone was quarried, transported and dressed. Egyptians may have used just limited amounts of limestone during the 1st and 2nd Dynasties.

The Step Pyramid Complex contains at least one million tons of stone. It is incredible that such a sudden increase in production could have been achieved in just one generation.

Why and how do you think this happened?

As stated earlier, because of their use of man-made stone instead of natural stone.

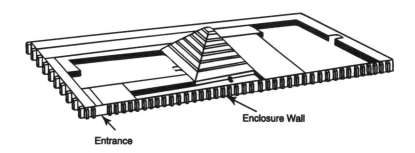

Entrance

Enclosure Wall

The Pyramid Complex of Zoser

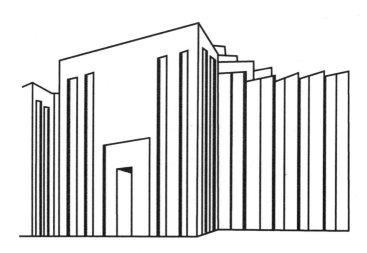

The Enclosure Wall of Zoser's Complex

The amount of stone used in the Zoser Complex (such as the enclosure wall) indicates mastery of stonemaking, before the time of Khufu (Cheops in Greek). Therefore, this Complex deserves more attention than the Great Pyramids of Giza.

Tell me about the enclosure wall.

The enclosure wall is a part of the Zoser Complex that King Zoser built. It surrounds an area more than a square mile. When complete, the enclosure wall was 1,000 cubits (nearly 600 yards, 549m) long, and 500 cubits (300 yards, 274m) wide, and rose to a height of over 30' (9.1m). It is built of limestone and faced with finely polished limestone.

The enclosure wall's successive recesses and projections required more than triple the amount of both stone and labor of a similarly-sized simple (flat) wall.

This enclosure wall has 14 bastion gates, but only one is real. The other 13 are simulated.

•   •   •

One can see the application of divine harmonic proportions (sacred geometry), more than 2,000 years before Plato and Pythagoras.

Yes, the Complex is a perfect double square, whose walls are oriented exactly along the cardinal directions.

This vast sanctuary set the pattern for later holy places, in Egypt and elsewhere.

This was a very active site for all successive Pharaohs. Among its major functions was to serve as the Heb-Sed site.

What is Heb-Sed?

Heb-Sed was the most important festival from the point of view of the Kingship. The empowerment of the King was renewed at this festival. The Heb-Sed Festival took place at regular intervals during the King's life.

The fertility of the soil, the abundant harvests, the health of people and cattle, the normal flow of events and all phenomena of life, were intimately linked to the potential of the ruler's vital force.

Being a divine medium, the Egyptian King was not supposed (or even able) to reign unless he was in good health.

The Heb-sed festival was a rejuvenation of this vital force (as per our common expression, he becomes "good as new").

•   •   •

Let us go through the only entrance. After going through this entrance, we walk through a beautiful colonnade. We then turn right and continue towards the Zoser Pyramid.

On the right-hand side one can notice fluted columns. These columns look the same as the well-known Doric columns of Greece.

Are these columns older than the Greek columns?

These Egyptian columns are at least 2,000 years older then the Greek columns. Calling them "Greek Doric columns" is a historical deception.

Who designed this complex?

He was known as Imhotep. He was Zoser's architect and vizier.

In the court of Zoser's Step Pyramid Complex stood a statue upon whose plinth was the name *Imhotep* with the citation, '*Chancellor of the King, First after the King, nobleman, High Priest of Onnu/Annu (Heliopolis), Builder, Sculptor, and Maker of Stone Vases in Chief*'.

Imhotep

This is an impressive list of official positions emphasizing the exceptional talent of this man.

Imhotep, above all others, stands at the head of the Western tradition of *sacred geometry*.

He also revolutionized the use of limestone in building.

He was the first to use stone of such large magnitude in building.

He is considered in history as the greatest father of masons.

So, his knowledge preceded that of the Greeks and the Romans?

His knowledge and wisdom were renowned for thousands of years. The Greeks called him Imuthes and identified him with their god Asclepius, son of Apollo.

Did they ever find his tomb?

Imhotep's own tomb has not been found — though hundreds of tombs of lesser individuals have been found and identified. Saqqara is a site that until now has been impossible to excavate thoroughly, because during the early days of archeology, every time an area was dug out, the sand was dumped on another area potentially no less rich in finds. It is therefore just possible that Imhotep's tomb may yet be found.

● ● ●

Let us go through the only entrance.

After going through the entrance, we walk through a beautiful colonnade. We then turn right and continue towards the Zoser Pyramid.

Δ Δ Δ

Pyramid #1
The Step Pyramid of Zoser

How did the idea of a pyramid come to Imhotep?

The idea of a step pyramid was not in his original plan. The original objective was to build a mastaba-type tomb to bury the king when he died.

Building a step pyramid was an afterthought, that occured a few years later. The mastaba-type tomb is functionally and structurally independent of the later addition of the stepped pyramid.

How did the mastaba-type tomb wind up to be the Step Pyramid of Zoser?

It occured over five stages of construction.

How did we figure out the construction stages of the Zoser Pyramid?

The stages of construction can be followed because almost all the outer casing has disappeared, as well as many layers of the core masonry. The eastern, southern, and north-

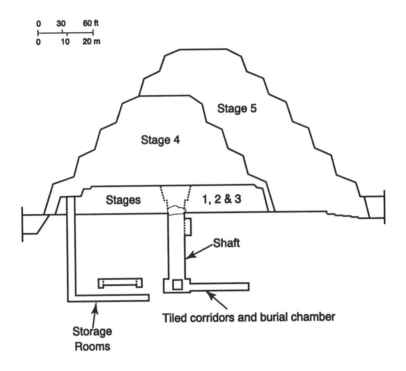

Height: 115 cubits (197' or 60m)
Base: 270 x 225 cubits (459' x 387' or 140m x 118m)

Zoser's Step Pyramid
Showing Stages of Construction

ern faces show clearly the five distinct construction stages.

Can you explain the five stages?

The **first stage** was the building of an unusual square stone mastaba 120 x 120 x 15 cubits (206' x 206' x 26') [63m x 63m x 8m] (others were rectangular), with an underground burial chamber. The core masonry was made of small stone blocks, laid like bricks. The stone mastaba was faced with fine limestone, which proves it was intended to be a finished building.

The **second stage** comprised the addition of 6 cubits (10', 3m) of fine limestone around the perimeter of the mastaba.

The **third stage** was the addition of a further 15 cubits (25', 7.5m) extension to the eastern face, providing a rectangular ground plan. An additional central shaft, a series of corridors and another tomb chamber were also dug.

The **fourth stage** was the construction of a four-tiered structure of stone, weighing 200,000 tons, on top of the existing tomb structure.

The **fifth stage** was the addition of two more steps and the final six-tiered pyramid, was, in turn, faced with fine limestone, to give it a smooth finish.

In simple terms, this structure is basically a mastaba-type tomb which was covered with a series of limestone steps.

Exactly. The main purpose of this structure was the burial of Zoser and his family. The Step Pyramid was an afterthought. The burial chambers are not an integral part of the pyramid structure.

Δ   Δ   Δ

Underground Chambers

What is this shaft?

At the bottom of the shaft, there are the burial chambers and a network of passages and small chambers, used for storing the funerary equipment and for the burials of Zoser and five members of his family.

The burial chambers of the Step Pyramid are burial chambers beyond any doubt. They contain inscriptions, offering rooms, and most of the other funerary features found in both earlier and later tombs. Some of these underground chambers are lined with beautiful blue faience tiles.

Did they know about faience tiles that long ago?

Yes. However, there are those who want to credit this invention to others in Europe. They claim, without any proof, that the walls were lined with these tiles much later than Zoser's time.

What is wrong with their claim?

Their claim is groundless. The so-called *"Southern Tomb"* (see page 79), just 700' (210m) from the Step Pyramid, and which was built during Zoser's reign, is lined with the very same tiles. The *"Southern Tomb"* was intact until it was discovered by the Egyptologists, Lauer and Firth, in 1924-26.

• • •

It is here, in some of these underground rooms, that the 40,000 items — including stone jars and vessels of every imaginable size, shape, and material — were found.

Pyramid #2
Sekhemket's Pyramid

West of the Unas Structure, we come to the Pyramid Complex of Sekhemket. In front of the ruins of this Pyramid Complex, we see stone blocks spread over a wide area.

What happened here?

Some claim that this pyramid was never finished. It is more logical to conclude that it was destroyed and hauled away by Moslem rulers, as occurred throughout Egypt.

From the size of its foundation, it appears that the finished step pyramid was to be seven steps, rising to a height of 230' (70m).

What is special about this pyramid?

There was no sign here of a central mastaba, as in the case of Zoser's Pyramid. The whole building was laid out, from the beginning, as a step pyramid.

Who built this pyramid?

It seems that this pyramid was built during the reign of

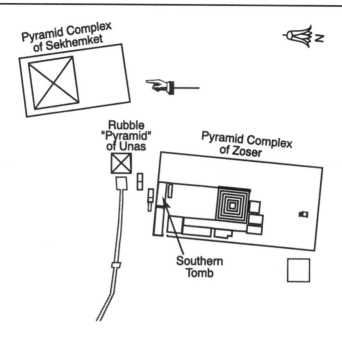

Saqqara Site Plan (Partial)

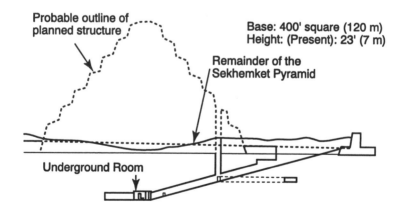

"Unfinished" Pyramid of Sekhemket

King Sekhemket (2611-2603 BCE). There is no direct evidence or any inscription or identification of Sekhemket or anybody else, inside the pyramid.

No identification. This is strange.

The mystery of the pyramids begins with Sekhemket because his and all subsequent masonry pyramids did not have any official inscriptions, whatsoever.

Do you think these blocks were man-made also?

Yes. The stone blocks here are similar in size to Zoser's pyramid. To confirm that the blocks were man-made, they found the Pharaoh's name (Sekhemket) on monuments in Sinai, near the mine sites of the arsenic minerals which are needed to make limestone blocks.

●   ●   ●

So, what did they find underneath this Pyramid?

Δ   There was no vertical shaft (like Zoser's), but there is an underground room, 98' (30m) deep, under the center of the pyramid.

Δ   Access to the underground room is via a sloping tunnel, with the entrance point located on the north side of the pyramid.

Δ   In this lone underground room, they found an uninscribed stone chest, consisting of a single hollow block of alabaster, which has an opening at one end, instead of a lid.

The opening was closed with a sliding door, also of alabaster, and sealed with cement that was unbroken. In May, 1954, the sliding door was raised and the stone chest turned out to be completely empty.

In short, the stone chest was found sealed in an undisturbed status, but empty.

Δ   There are no inscriptions whatsoever in the underground room or on the stone chest.

Did they find other things underneath this pyramid?

Actually, they did. They found a door framed by an arch.

An arch? So long ago?

Yes. Its existence proves to the world that ancient Egyptians invented and used arches thousands of years before the Greeks and Romans did.

Zawyet el Aryan

We have just traveled 6 miles (10 km) north of Saqqara, to Zawyet el Aryan, where we will visit Pyramid #3.
We are now in front of the ruins of Kha-ba's Pyramid.
We see stone blocks spread over a wide area.
Some claim that this pyramid was never finished. It is more logical to conclude that it was destroyed and hauled away by Moslem rulers, as occurred throughout Egypt.

Who built this pyramid?

It appears that this pyramid was built during the reign of King Kha-ba (2603-2599 BCE). There are no inscriptions whatsoever, inside or outside the structure, which identify Kha-ba or anyone else as the builder. A reference to Kha-ba's name is found in the nearby cemetery, which made him the most likely builder.

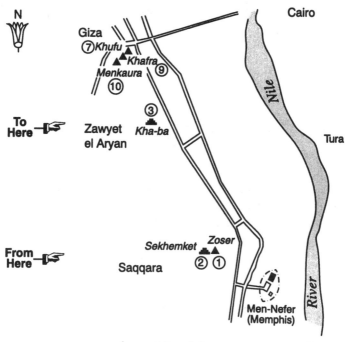

Location Map

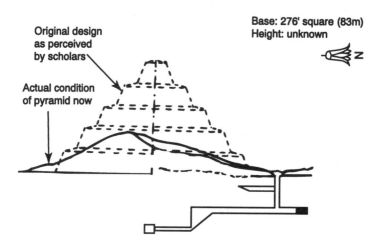

Base: 276' square (83m)
Height: unknown

Original design
as perceived
by scholars

Actual condition
of pyramid now

The Pyramid of Kha-ba

He used small blocks just like Zoser and Sekhemket.

Very much so. The blocks are just slightly larger here.

Was the final structure intended to be a stepped pyramid?

Yes. It is actually known as the *Layer Pyramid.* Like the Sekhemket Pyramid, the structure here has no central mastaba-type tomb. The whole building was laid out, from the beginning, as a step pyramid.

What is underneath this pyramid?

There is only one empty underground room. The passage to the underground room, is located on the north face of the pyramid. The interior is inaccessible at this time.

There was no sarcophagus or stone chest anywhere.

Δ   Δ   Δ

We travel south now,
about 40 miles (65 km)
to

Meidum

where we will visit
Pyramid #4.

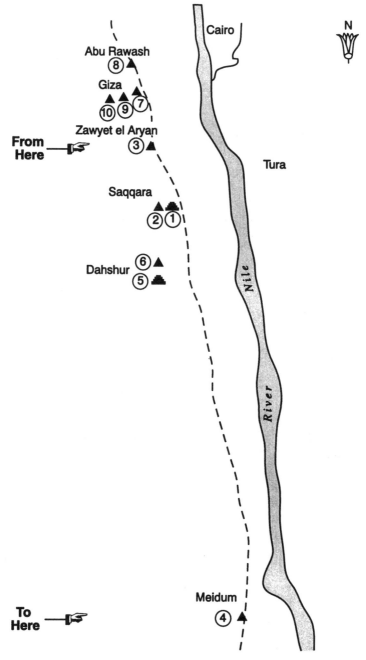

Location Map of the Ten Pyramids

Meidum

Pyramid #4
Snefru's Meidum
Pyramid

Pyramid #4 is the most southern masonry pyramid. As we get closer to Meidum, we see the outline of a strange structure.

What is this structure?

This is the remains of a pyramid.

It does not look like a pyramid at all.

True. It looks more like kind of a high, stepped tower, rising out of a tremendous heap of rubble.

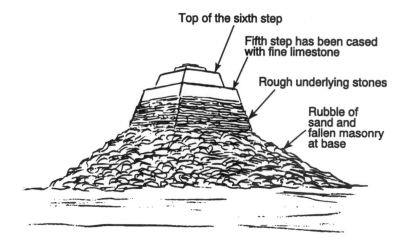

The Collapsed Pyramid of Meidum

Who built it?

There are no inscriptions indicating who built it. King Huni's name is not mentioned anywhere in the area. Several graffiti on and around the ruins indicate that the Egyptians themselves ascribed it to King Snefru (2575-2551 BCE). Despite this fact, some people guessed that the pyramid was built, or mostly built, by Huni (2599-2575 BCE), last of the 3rd Dynasty Kings.

Was it both kings who built it then?

All circumstantial evidence indicates that Snefru alone built it. But the people who insist that the pyramids were tombs and nothing else, could not deal with Snefru having three pyramids which, in their minds, means three tombs. This is the reason they came up with the unfounded story — that Huni built (or mostly built) this pyramid.

How was this pyramid built?

The original plan of this structure was to build a step pyramid, and was later converted into a true pyramid with smooth sides. So, historically this is the first known true pyramid.

It was built in three phases. Each phase was intended to be final because the exterior walls of each phase had a finished fine limestone dressing.

The *first phase* consisted of building a seven-tiered step pyramid, and it was finished by the customary casing of fine-grained limestone. It was 196' (60m) high.

The *second phase* consisted of adding an eighth step, which received another layer of casing stones. The height then became 262' (80 m).

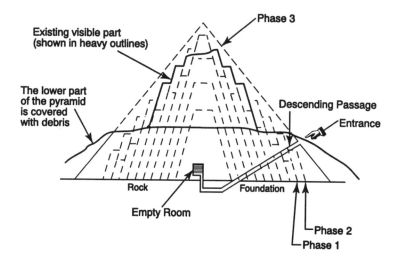

Height (original): 306' (93m)
Mass (original?): 1.5 million tons
Base (original): 482' (147m) square
Angle: 51° 50' 35"

The Meidum Pyramid of Snefru

The *third phase* transformed the eight-tiered step pyramid into a true pyramid with smooth sides. Packing blocks were added and a final layer of casing stones was laid at a steep inward angle, to overcome the side pressure of successive courses of masonry.

How did the pyramid end up to be the way it is now?

After the pyramid was completed, a few of the casing blocks were squeezed out of place, a chain reaction followed, and the entire outer casing gave way. Much of the core masonry was pulled with the loose casing stones. As a result of this avalanche, a huge rubble heap was formed around the pyramid, which left portions of the earlier step pyramid intact. This explains its towerlike appearance.

How do you know that the collapse occurred after the pyramid was completed and not during the pyramid construction?

The presence of the Pyramid Temple (wrongly known as a *mortuary* temple), next to the collapsed pyramid, proves that the collapse occurred after the pyramid was completed. They would not have built this temple next to the pyramid, if the pyramid actually collapsed during construction. To build a temple next to a collapsed pyramid, would have been a moot and dangerous undertaking.

This collapsed pyramid that looks like a tower reminds me of the Tower of Babel. Any connection?

The biblical tale of the fall of the Tower of Babel was probably a garbled folk memory of the collapse of the Meidum Pyramid. It was also believed that the original seven steps of the pyramid conformed to the seven planets and their associated seven musical sounds. The additional eighth step was contrary to sacred scripts and may have been the reason it collapsed.

Any geometric significance to this (first known true) pyramid?

It has the same geometric distinctions (but with different dimensions) to the later-built **Khufu**'s Pyramid, i.e. the angle between the face and the base of the pyramid.

The blocks of this pyramid are larger than the previous three pyramids. Right?

Yes. Some of its blocks weigh about 550 pounds (250kg).

There is no evidence of these stone blocks being quarried locally or otherwise. On the other hand, records in the mines of Sinai indicate vigorous activities during Snefru's reign. Again showing that arsenic minerals, needed for the production of man-made limestone blocks, were extracted.

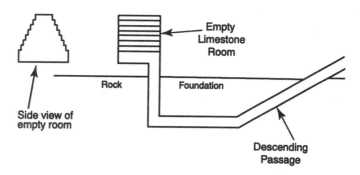

How about the interior rooms?

There is only one small room, with no inscriptions, which

has a fine corbelled roof (fashioned like steps in reverse), composed of seven steps, to look like the original intent of the pyramid's seven steps. Incidentally, the Grand Gallery in the later-built Khufu's Great Pyramid of Giza has an identical design.

Access to the room in the Meidum Pyramid can only be achieved from the corridor via a narrow vertical shaft. The interior room is set at the top of the shaft. This vertical shaft enters the floor of the room and is only 3.8' x 2.8' (117 x 85cm) wide.

No sarcophagus or stone chest?

None. Totally empty. There was never a stone chest there, because it would have had to be placed in the room at the time when it was being built, and it could not have left the room by the narrow shaft, except if broken into pieces. No granite fragments of a stone chest were found, either in the room itself or anywhere in the corridor.

●   ●   ●

What are the general characteristics of the Pyramid Complexes during the 4ᵗʰ Dynasty?

1.   From the Meidum Pyramid onward, the entrance to all masonry pyramids was well above ground. The interior rooms were mostly located at the base of the pyramid itself.

2.   This and all subsequent masonry pyramids share the same pattern of noticeably low and narrow passages, which lack adequate space to move around, or stand up straight.

3.   The narrow entrance passage is at a slope of 1:2, which

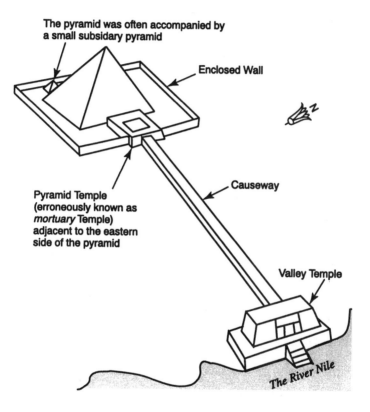

The pyramid was often accompanied by
a small subsidary pyramid

Enclosed Wall

Pyramid Temple
(erroneously known as
mortuary Temple)
adjacent to the eastern
side of the pyramid

Causeway

Valley Temple

The River Nile

Classical Pyramid Complex

makes the passage at the diagonal of the sacred double square.

4. A small enclosure and a pyramid temple (erroneously known as *mortuary*) with a causeway to the river, was repeated in all the subsequent pyramids.

Δ   Δ   Δ

Next, we retrace our travels
to the north, about 30 miles
(50 km), to

Dahshur

where we will visit
Pyramid #5
and
Pyramid #6.

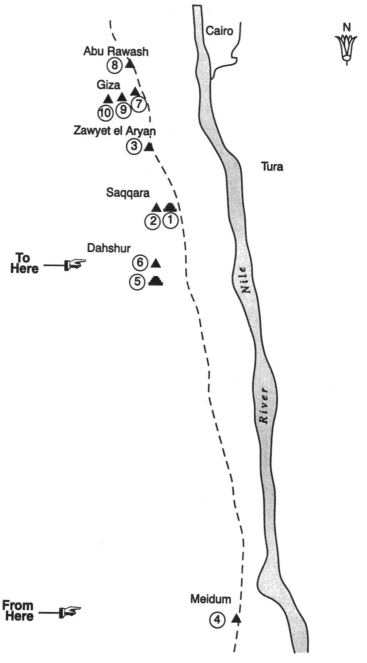

Location Map of the Ten Pyramids

Dahshur

Pyramid #5
Snefru's Bent Pyramid

The Bent Pyramid alone has a double-angled profile, and two totally separate sets of rooms, one entrance on the customary north side, and a second entrance on the west side.

Who built this pyramid?

As is the case in the prior three pyramids, this pyramid is again totally void of any markings.

This pyramid was attributed to King Snefru (2575-2551 BCE), based on a reference to his name in the nearby temple.

Why are there two angles of inclination for this pyramid?

The evidence inside the Bent Pyramid leads us to conclude

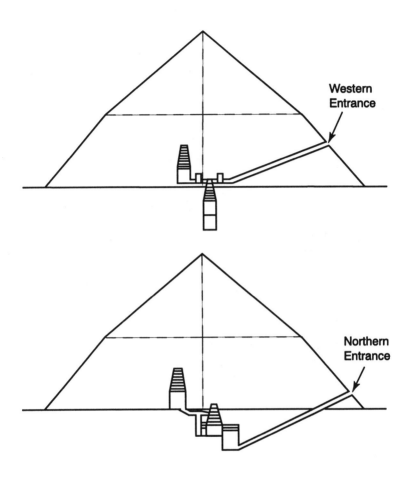

Base:	602' (184m) square
Height:	344' (105m)
Mass:	3.6 million tons
Inclination:	53° 27' base
	43° 22' 44" top

Snefru's Bent Pyramid

that its unique double angle was a deliberately planned design since:

△   The early stages of construction reflected that these separate entrances, corridors, and underground rooms were part of the original plan.

△   The emphasis upon a dual purpose or dual symbolism for this pyramid seems more reasonable than attempting to explain it as yet another change of plan.

△   The French Egyptologist, Varille, stated that two slopes for each side of this pyramid had been designed this way intentionally, with the aim of obtaining a certain geometrical ratio between the ground-level section and the middle section of the pyramid.

What is inside the pyramid?

△   The descending passage from the northern entrance is 3'-7" (1.1m) high. Again, like Meidum, the passage is too small for any person to walk up straight, and it follows the diagonal of a 1:2 rectangle.

△   The passageway leads to two internal rooms, which have corbel roofs. There is no trace of a stone chest or of a burial taking place in either room.

△   A second passage connects the upper room with an opening high up in the western face of the pyramid. This passageway is also 3'-7" (1.1m) high, which is too small for standing up.

The blocks here vary in size, don't they?

Yes, such variety in sizes provides for better interlocking, which ensures the stability of the structure.

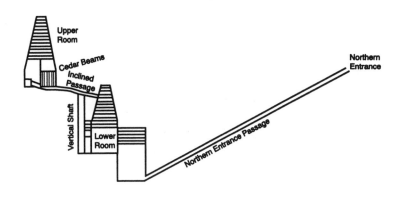

Profile View

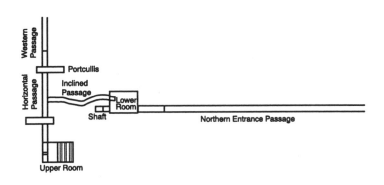

Plan View (Bird's Eye View)

Passages and Rooms in
the Bent Pyramid at Dahshur

Pyramid #6
Snefru's Red Pyramid

We now proceed to another pyramid less than a mile (1.6 km) north of the Bent Pyramid, which is called the *Northern Pyramid of Dahshur*.

It is popularly known as the *Red Pyramid* because of the reddish or pinkish tint of its core stones.

This pyramid is in good condition.

This is the earliest monument that is in complete pyramidical form. It looks good because it still retains large areas of its original casing stones.

Who built this pyramid?

Again, there are no inscriptions whatsoever inside or outside of this pyramid. It is believed that this pyramid was built during the reign of King Snefru (2575-2551 BCE).

Any interesting geometric features?

Yes, the inclination of the face of the pyramid is exactly like the upper section of the Bent Pyramid.

Height: 341' (104m)
Base: 722' square (220m)
Mass: 4.0 million tons
Inclination: 43° 22' 44"

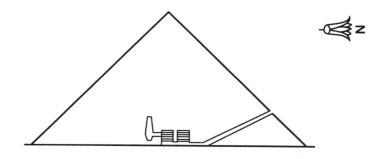

Snefru's Red Pyramid

What is inside this pyramid?

Δ   The entrance passage is again the unique typical diagonal
of a 1:2 rectangle. It leads down a long, sloping corridor,
to the bedrock, and is only 3'-11" (1.2m) high, i.e. too
small for a person to walk standing up straight.

Δ   The passage leads to two adjoining identical rooms with
the typical corbelled roofs.

Δ   A short passage leads upward to a third large room. The
corbelled roof of this third room rises to a height of 50'
(15.2m).

The rooms here were also empty?

Yes. No inscriptions and traces of a stone chest or burial
were found anywhere in the three rooms.

Really unique arrangement.

It sure is. Also here, for the first time, the rooms were incorporated into the pyramid itself (traditionally they were located at the base of the pyramid itself).

The blocks here are huge!

Yes. The height of blocks here vary from 1'-7" (.5m) to 4'-7" (1.4m).

So, Snefru built several large pyramids.

Yes. Snefru built three colossal pyramids, and erected stone monuments throughout Egypt. It is estimated that nine million tons of stone were used during the Pharaoh's 24-year reign.

Snefru

And Snefru used more stone in building than the famous Khufu?

Yes. Building with stone occurred on a much larger scale prior to the building of **Khufu**'s Great Pyramid at Giza.

Let us not forget the big project of the Zoser Complex at Saqqara.

So, Snefru was never buried in his pyramids?

There is no evidence of burial in any of the three pyramids. It should be clearer than ever that these pyramids were not built to entomb anybody.

Ungenuine "Pyramids" of Dahshur

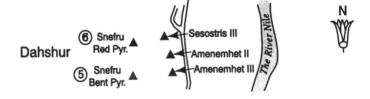

Are there other pyramids in Dahshur?

There are ungenuine "pyramids", which belong to Ame-nemhet II (1929-1892 BCE), Sesostris III (1878-1844 BCE), and Amenemhet III (1844-1797 BCE).

Each was made of a core of crude mud-brick, surrounded by an outer casing of limestone, now disappeared. Presently, they are just shapeless masses.

Couldn't these Pharaohs afford to build stone masonry pyramids?

The economical situation during the reigns of both Amenemhet III and Sesostris III was excellent. They both built extensively in stone throughout Egypt.

Were they buried under these cheap "pyramids"?

Yes they were. It is very clear that the inner structures of these later ungenuine "pyramids" are totally different than those interiors in the older nine masonry pyramids. These ungenuine ones have the regular spacious passages and funerary inscriptions, etc., just like all the other tombs in ancient Egypt.

Δ   Δ   Δ

Next, we continue to retrace
our travels north, about 15
miles (25 km), from
Dahshur to

Giza

where we will discuss
Pyramid #7.

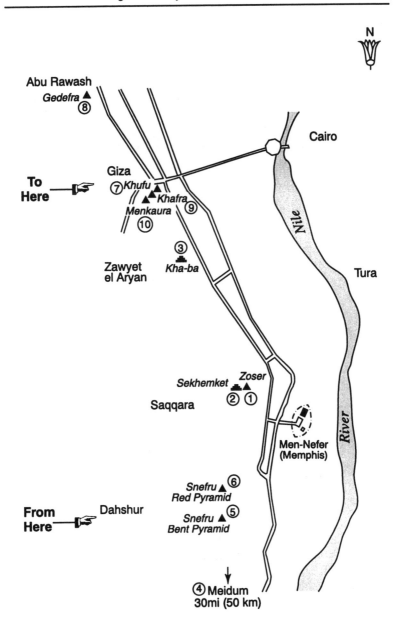

Map of the Ten Pyramids
Numbered in their Chronological Order

The Giza Plateau

The Giza Plateau is an enormous and impressive site. Our main focus now will be the three Giza pyramids.

1	Great Pyramid of Khufu (Cheops).
2	Tomb of Queen Hetepheres.
3	Mastaba fields.
4	Pyramid of Khafra (Chephren).
5	Pyramid Temple of Khafra.
6	Causeway to Valley Temple.
7	Great Sphinx.
8	Temple of the Sphinx.
9	Valley Temple of Khafra.
10	Pyramid of Menkaura (Mycerinus).
11	Pyramid Temple of Menkaura.
12	Menkaura Causeway.
13	Valley Temple of Menkaura.

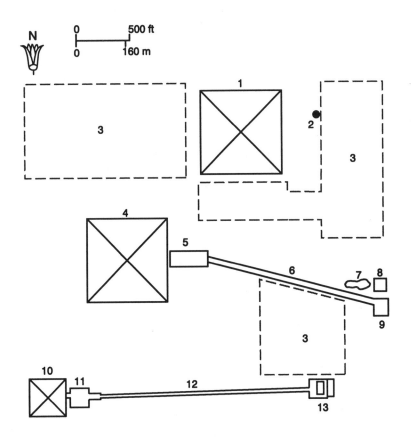

The Giza Plateau

The Exterior

This is an awesome structure.

The Great Pyramid of **Khufu** is the largest of all the pyramids.

It should be noted that its geometric relationship between the four faces and the base are the same as the Collapsed Pyramid of Snefru at Meidum.

Additional information includes:

Δ   Its base area is approximately 13 acres (53,000 sq. meters), enough to hold the cathedrals of Florence, Milan and St. Peters, as well as Westminster Abbey and St. Paul's.

Δ   The sides of its base are lined up almost exactly with the cardinal points of the compass. The average discrepancy of alignment is only 3'-6" (0.06%).

Δ   The length of the sides of the base vary within 0.08% accuracy limit.

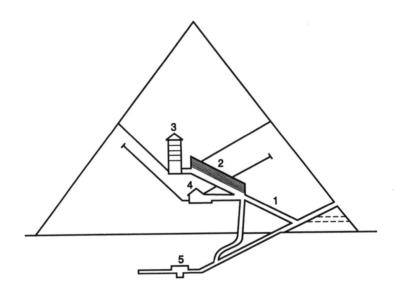

1. Ascending Passage
2. Grand Gallery
3. "King's" Room
4. "Queen's" Room
5. Subterranean Room

Height (Original):	280 cubits (481', 147m)
Base:	440 cubits square (757' sq, 229m sq)
Mass:	6.5 million tons of limestone
Area of base:	13 acres (5.3 hectares)
Inclination:	51° 50' 35"

Khufu's Pyramid

☞ The degrees of accuracy, in orientation towards the cardinal points, keeping the base square and the perfection of the four sloping sides, are incredible, considering the size of the structure.

Can you explain the harmonic proportion of this pyramid?

The very small variations [of several inches over the 754' length (230m) of the base] were deliberate. They were meant to incorporate into the pyramid the "discrepancies" of the earth itself, which is the flattening of the earth's globe at the poles. As a result, they incorporated both ratios into the pyramid. With such intended construction, the Egyptians were able to embody in the pyramid's shape both:
- the **Neb** (Golden) Proportion (so-called ϕ)
- the Circle Index (so-called π)

The angle of the slope of each face is considered to be 51° 50' 35". This would indicate it being built according to the Circle Index and the height being the perimeter divided by double the Circle Index. If the angle is 51° 49' 38", the **Neb** (Golden) Proportion would be implicated and the apothem would be half the base length times the **Neb** (Golden) Proportion. In reality, this involved inches in difference, which is the case here, and as such both the Proportion and Index are reflected in the external dimensions of this pyramid.

Do we have clues from earlier travelers and historians?

Herodotus was told by the temple priests that the Great Pyramid was constructed in such a way that the area of each face was equal to the square of its height. This relationship can be seen to embody the **Neb** (Golden) Proportion.

Herodotus' reports are further corroborated by the actual dimensions in the ancient Egyptian units of cubits: 280 for the original height and 440 for the side of the base. The ratio of these two figures [280/220 = h/b = 14/11] corresponds to the square root of the **Neb** (Golden) Proportion.

There is a surprising bonus. Divide twice the base by the height and you get 3.14, a practically perfect value of the Circle Index.

A theoretical "value" of the Circle Index (3.1415927) is useless. If you cannot measure and/or build to such a meaningless fraction, it is a waste of time to calculate it.

Incorporating the Circle Index into the Pyramid's design is also significant?

The angle of elevation of 51° 50' 35", expresses the Circle Index (22/7) with very considerable precision. The angle of ascent gives the pyramid a unique geometrical property that represents the mystic squaring of the circle: that the ratio of the pyramid's perimeter to its height is equal to double the Circle Index.

What is the significance of squaring the circle?

I will give you a quick answer, but a more elaborate explanation and background can be found in the book, *Egyptian Harmony: The Visual Music*, ISBN 0-9652509-8-9.

The circle in ancient Egypt was the symbol for **Ra**, representing the Absolute, or undifferentiated unity. As such, ancient Egyptians rarely use the circle in their monuments.

In ancient Egypt, wherever there was a problem that required obtaining the area of a circle, they consistently squared the circle. The square represents the physical manifestation of the metaphysical circle.

So, the ancient Egyptians knew these important (irrational) numbers so early in history.

"Irrational numbers" is a wrong but common term. The Neb (Golden) Proportion and the Circle Index were seen by the ancient Egyptians not in numerical terms but as emblematical of the creative or generative function, the fundamental of an infinite series, i.e. the Summation (so-called *Fibonacci*) Series. One cannot just reduce a process/function to a meaningless, unmeasurable "value". These are functions representing a ratio/proportion between independent but related parts/function.

This, however, is not the first time that the ancient Egyptians used these important relationships, because Snefru's Pyramid at Meidum has the same geometric characteristics as Khufu's Pyramid.

This is a wonderful implementation of Divine Harmonic Proportions (sacred geometry).

Could incorporating these functions have been just coincidental?

Of course not. Their application of this knowledge was consistent throughout — at least 3,000 years. People who don't want to be outshined by the ancient Egyptians will go to such extremes as to insist that this geometrical relationship had to be accidental. They claim that the builders of the pyramid laid out its dimensions by rolling a drum along the ground.

Did they?

There is no evidence whatsoever that the Egyptians ever measured anything by rolling a drum. The Egyptians laid out their temples by a well-known and often depicted method called *stretching the cord.*

Is it even possible to use a drum for measuring linear distances?

This is a sheer invention by people who can't stand the advanced knowledge of the ancient Egyptians.

Additionally, any logical person cannot expect that such an imaginary drum just happened to stop rolling at 377' (115m), which is the center of the Great Pyramid. And nobody could expect such a rolling drum to yield dimensions within a few millimeters of accurary, 1/8 of one degree of the earth's latitude at the equator.

Δ   Δ   Δ

What are the main construction features of this pyramid?

Δ   The pyramid consists of 203 steps. The heights of the steps continually decrease from bottom to top. However, there are hundreds of blocks weighing from 15 to 30 tons situated near the "King's" Room. Blocks of this size are so large that they occupy the space of two tiers.

Δ   The pyramid was surrounded by and built partly upon a pavement or platform of limestone blocks, portions of which can be seen at the northern and eastern sides.

Δ   Δ   Δ

The Builders

Who built this pyramid?

The building of this pyramid is attributed to King **Khnum-Khufu**, who is generally known as Khufu (Cheops in Greek), and who reigned from 2551-2528 BCE.

Khnum-Khufu

Khnum-Khufu, not just Khufu?

This is significant, because **Khnum**, as explained earlier, represents the Divine Molder. This is significant because it relates to the method of making stones by molding/casting them.

What is the evidence that Khnum-Khufu build this pyramid?

1.   The inscriptions in the mastabas surrounding the pyramid make several references to the name of **Khnum-Khufu**.

2.   The Greek historian, Herodotus, attributed this pyramid to **Khnum-Khufu**, based on the information provided to him by his priest informants.

Was Khnum-Khufu a good Pharaoh?

The alleged "tyranny of Cheops (**Khufu**)" cited by the Greek historian Herodotus (c. 500 BCE), was generally accepted, and even elaborated upon, by non-factual writers.

What is wrong with such a notion?

Firstly, there is no evidence to suggest that people were compelled to work against their will. Indeed, if anything, the opposite is more probable. Upon rational reflection, it is reasonable to suppose that they labored willingly. This is not hard to comprehend once the notion of the pyramid being a tomb is dismissed. The sheer quality of craftsmanship in the construction of the pyramids suggests a pride in the work.

Secondly, rational scholars challenged the notion of slave labor, since managing such huge numbers of disgruntled slaves, gathered in one small area, would have been a potentially explosive task.

Thirdly, the unfounded theory that the pyramid blocks were cut, transported, and hoisted into position, are indicative of harsh working conditions.

As explained earlier, such a theory is wrong on all accounts. A much smaller workforce was used, to manufacture the man-made blocks.

Fourthly, Herodotus reported that his Egyptian guide told him that Khufu's predecessor, Snefru, was a good King. Yet the three mighty pyramids at Dahshur and Meidum, attributed to Snefru, required much more stones and labor than that required for the Great Pyramid itself. This is a major contradiction in Herodotus' account of the "*tyrant*" and "*good*" kings.

Herodotus was relating information that has been transferred by word-of-mouth, over a span of 2,000 years. One should expect some inconsistencies.

Lastly, the role of the Pharaoh was not to rule/govern, but to be the medium between the people and the supernatural forces, for the benefit of the health and well-being of the land and people.

Khufu's Great Pyramid

The Interior

Entering the Pyramid

As with all the other pyramids, the entrance is on the north side.

Why is this entrance so rough looking?

This is actually the entrance of the forced passage. The original entrance is that aperture beneath the huge limestone gables, located higher up and to the left of the forced entrance.

Why didn't they use the original entrance, which is only a short distance from the forced entry?

Δ   The true entrance was covered with stone blocks for thousands of years, and therefore was invisible.

Δ   People had been trying to enter the pyramid, for thousands of years, looking for possible gold and treasures.

Δ   The Arab Caliph, Al Mamun, in the 9th century, unaware of the original entrance, forced his way through the solid stone, in the sixth course of masonry, which led him to the first interior passage of the pyramid. Only then, by tracking this interior passage, was he able to find the location of the true original entrance. The stone blocks, covering the entrance, were then removed.

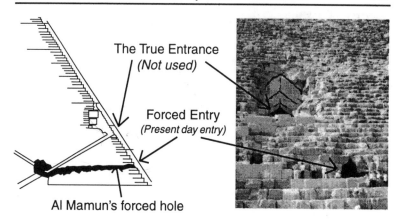

The True Entrance
(Not used)

Forced Entry
(Present day entry)

Al Mamun's forced hole

The Two Entries

That must have been hard work, for Al Mamun, to cut through the stones.

It sure looks like it. The passage which Al Mamun cut was 118' (36m) long before he reached the junction of the original descending and ascending passages.

Are you saying nobody before Al Mamun had access to the interior of the pyramid?

That's correct. There is no evidence whatsoever, either on the outer surfaces of the pyramid or inside it, that suggests that someone had broken into the pyramid earlier.

Did any ancient historian refer to the interior passageways?

Herodotus did not mention any passages. The Greco/Roman historian, Strabo (1st century CE) reported that the pyramid entrance was concealed behind a secret stone, indistinguishable from the others.

The Descending Passage and Subterranean Room

△ At the end of Al Mamun's forced passageway, one reaches the pyramid's descending passage, which starts from the original and only intended entrance to the pyramid.

△ This descending passage runs exactly north-south (i.e. it is meridional).

△ The slope of the descending corridor corresponds to the diagonal of a 1:2 rectangle.

Where does the descending passage end?

It goes down below the base of the pyramid and into the bedrock, to the *Subterranean Room*.

This passage is very narrow.

It sure is, as was the case in all pyramids after Zoser. It is only 3'-6" (1.1m) wide, and 3'-11" (1.2m) high.

How long is this descending passage?

The passage is 345' (105m) long, plus the 29' (8.83m) horizontal corridor to where the Subterranean Room is located.

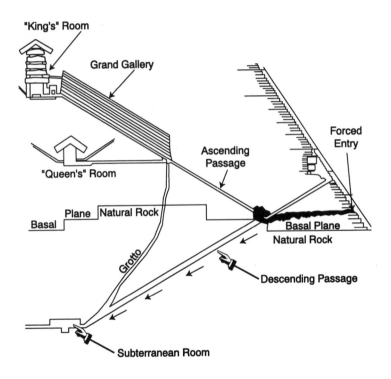

Khufu's Pyramid (partial view)

What is down there?

The Subterranean Room is located 600' (183m) below the apex of the pyramid. It is a very crude room, void of any inscriptions. It measures about 46' x 27'-1" x 11'-6" (14 x 8.3 x 3.5 m). Nobody knows the purpose of it, but that didn't stop many from making up answers.

What was said about this Subterranean Room?

Some theorize that it was intended to bury the King. And that the Egyptians changed the plan, abandoned it, and chose what is now the *"Queen's" Room*. Then these same people theorized again about another *change in plan*, in which the Egyptians abandoned the *"Queen's" Room* for the *"King's" Room*.

What do you think?

Δ   There is no evidence, physical or otherwise, that there was any *change in plan*, any place in this pyramid.

Δ   It is possible that this room was built for a specific purpose and was not simply an abandoned plan.

Δ   It could be that this room was in existence before the pyramid was even built.

What could be the purpose for this room?

There are many places in the ancient Egyptian monuments, where you will find friezes and rooms which were left totally or partially completed, for reasons unknown to us at the present time.

Did Herodotus mention this Subterranean Room?

Well, not quite.

According to Herodotus' account, the body of Khufu was placed in a room deep below the pyramid, and that the water from a canal, leading from the Nile, turned this room into an underground island.

No trace of such a room has ever been found. If it existed at the Nile level, it would have been found almost a hundred feet below the level of the present *Subterranean Room* — i.e. it would have to be cut 200' (60m) into the bedrock, below the base of the pyramid.

Did they find the room which Herodotus mentioned?

It was never found.

Why did Herodotus mention it then?

He was only reporting what someone told him, 2,000 years after the pyramid was built. Information via word of mouth, over a time span of sixty generations, could be partially or totally inaccurate. There is also the possibility of miscommunication/misunderstanding between any two parties (such as Herodotus and the Egyptian informants).

Δ   Δ   Δ

Ascending Passage

Which way shall we go now?

Δ   We have no choice but to go up the ascending passage. Take care not to bump your head on the low ceiling. This passage is only 3'-11" (1.2m) high, and 3'-6" (1.1m) wide, and rises at a 26½° angle (2:1 typical slope). It is only 129' (39m) long, but it will seem much longer, when you're going through this confining passageway.

Δ   This ascending passage runs exactly in a north-south direction i.e. it is meridional.

Δ   The walls are void of any inscriptions and/or drawings, like the previous pyramids after Zoser's.

It is too low and narrow to walk up straight.

It surely is. Can you imagine the situation with no wooden ramps or railings? The original floor is very slippery. With the inevitable sand on top of the floor, it would be almost impossible to keep oneself from sliding the whole way down.

In the 1940s, handrails and wooden ramps with metal footings were installed. It is also electrically lit inside, these days.

All the pyramids after Zoser's lack adequate space arrangements for maneuvering.

Δ   Δ   Δ

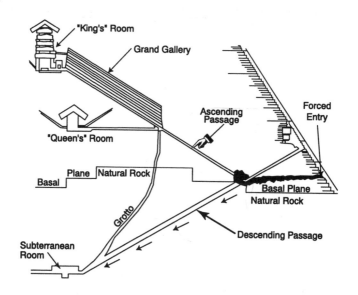

Khufu's Pyramid (partial view)

Up the low, narrow, and steep ascending passage with help of modern ramps and railings.

"Queen's" Room Corridor

At the juncture of the ascending and horizontal passages, is an opening of a shaft, which descends partly vertically and partly at a very steep angle to a depth of 197' (60m). It opens into the lower part of the descending passage.

Let us continue in the horizontal passage where it ends, at the so-called "*Queen's Room*".

This is hard on the back. It is too small again.

Yes. The low and narrow passage is only 3'-11" (1.2m) high, and 3'-6" (1.1m) wide.

The corridor is 127' (39m) long, and is located in the central mass of the core masonry.

Don't let your guard down. You will notice the floor dropping 1'-7" (0.5m) towards the end of the passage.

What is the purpose of this sudden drop?

This is another mystery, but we know these Egyptians did every little thing for a reason and/or a purpose.

I heard that the reason for this drop is a change in plan by the builders.

A "change in plan" is the academic standard "escape route" when they don't understand something. Academicians are incapable of saying "I don't know".

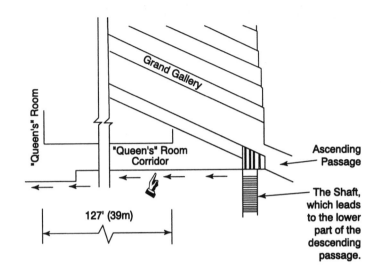

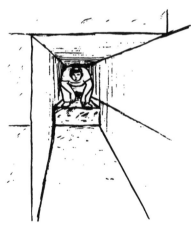

The mysterious sudden
drop in the passageway
to the "Queen's" Room

Crawling inside the
"Queen's" Room corridor

The "Queen's" Room

We enter a room that is made entirely of limestone walls with plaster over them. The floor has been left rough.

This room lies exactly on the pyramid's east-west axis.

Was the room always empty like this?

Yes, and all the scholars agree that nobody was ever buried here.

Why did they call it the *Queen's Room*?

The Arabs named it that way, because it reminded them of their tombs for women. The Arabs buried their women in rooms with gabled roofs, and men in rooms with flat roofs. Since this room has a gabled roof, they called it the *Queen's Room*.

Is that it? You can't be serious. It is so dumb, it is comical. That explains why you always say "so-called," when you refer to this room. By the way, what was the purpose of this room, then?

We don't know. The walls were and are totally bare. Some suggested that this room was built to bury the King and then the Egyptians changed their plan for the second time. The first time was the Subterranean Room below the base of the pyramid.

Is there any basis to this "change in plan" theory?

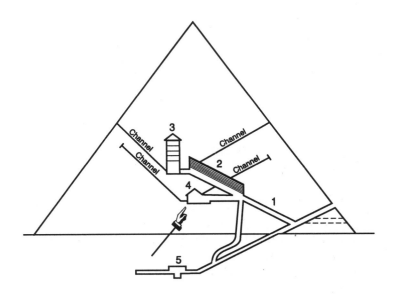

1. Ascending Passage
2. Grand Gallery
3. "King's" Room
4. "Queen's" Room
5. Subterranean Room

Khufu's Pyramid

No basis whatsoever. On the contrary, the physical evidence contradicts such a wild notion. We have two small and long channels here, which are known incorrectly as *air shafts*. They are about 8" x 8" (20cm x 20cm) in cross-section. Both channels are sealed at both ends. These channels were added to the core masonry, level by level as the pyramid went up.

If the Egyptians abandoned this room for what is now called the *"King's" Room*, there was no reason whatsoever to extend the channels of the *"Queen's" Room* beyond the floor level of the *"King's" Room*. But they did.

The southern channel was extended 64' (19.5 m) higher than the floor level of the *"King's" Room*, i.e. running almost parallel to the southern channel of the *"King's" Room* for 82' (25 m) of its track.

If these channels were not for ventilation, what is their purpose?

Δ   The two channels, one directed to the north and the other to the south, do not run through to the outside of the pyramid, proving that they were not intended to ventilate the room, as some have supposed.

Δ   They were called *"ventilation shafts"* because nobody knew what else to call them.

How about the northern channel?

The northern channel has many kinks in it because it goes around the Grand Gallery.

Was there a mistake then in the alignment of the northen channel?

Not at all, because the same situation occured again at the *"King's" Room*, several courses above the *"Queen's" Room*.

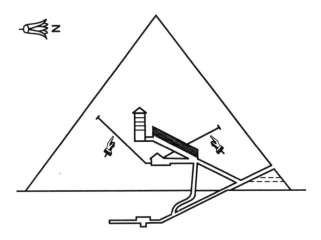

Orientation of the two channels in the "Queen's" Chamber

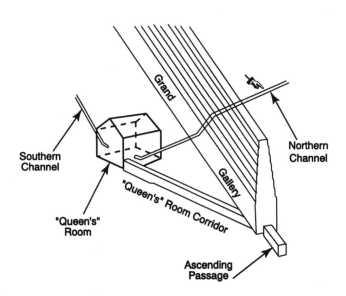

Kink in Northern Channel

The Grand Gallery

The Grand Gallery is reached after going back, through the horizontal corridor, towards the end of the ascending passage.

We can walk standing up in the Grand Gallery.

Δ   Yes, plenty of spare room.

Δ   Like all internal passages, the slope of this gallery is the diagonal of a 1:2 rectangle. The gallery is 157' (48m) long, 29' (85m) high, and 62" (1.6m) wide at the bottom, and 41" (1m) wide at the top, with a corbelled roof design (7 of them just like the Meidum Pyramid).

Δ   In the center of the floor is a sunken ramp about 2' (60cm) deep, which leads to the *"Queen's" Room.*

Again, I have yet to see any drawings and/or inscriptions on the walls, anywhere in the pyramid.

Exactly. This, and the other eight major pyramids, don't have any markings whatsoever.

This wooden ramp placed over the polished and smooth floor is making it much easier to climb.

Without it, it would be impossible to walk up the smooth, sloped surface.

•   •   •

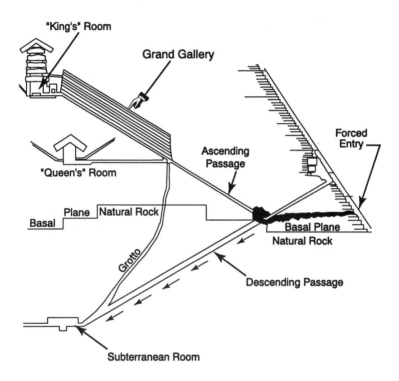

Khufu's Pyramid (Partial)

Immediately before one reaches the upper end of the Gallery, there is a 3' (1m) step, then it levels off.

At the top of the southern wall (upper end of the Gallery) is a small opening that leads to a forced passage, made to reach the area referred to as *Davison's Room*, atop the granite roof of the *"King's" Room*.

●　●　●

At the upper end of the Gallery, this very spacious and gorgeous Grand Gallery ended, and it was time to crawl on hands and knees again, towards the *"King's" Room*.

Δ　Δ　Δ

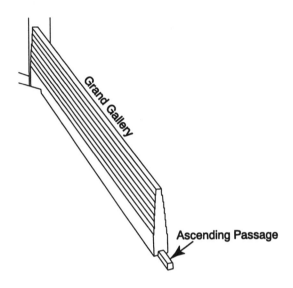

The Grand Gallery, The Masonry Telescope

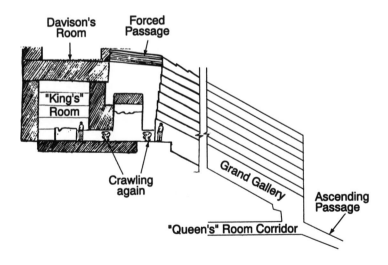

The Grand Gallery, Leading to the "King's" Room

The "King's" Room

Once again, it it time to crawl on hands and knees through a horizontal granite passageway, leading from the top end of the Grand Gallery, to the *"King's" Room.*

Remind me again, about Herodotus. He never mentioned this room, right?

He never mentioned any rooms or passageways in the pyramid.

This room is constructed entirely of monoliths of smooth granite.

The walls here are formed of five courses, containing exactly one hundred granite blocks.

Each monolith weighs 30 tons and all these blocks are perfectly smooth-faced. No mortar was used to join them. They are so perfectly fitted that a knife could not pass between them. This is incredible, for such a weight and such a fit.

The ceiling is formed of nine immense monoliths, some of them weighing over 50 tons.

What is above the roof of this room?

Δ   Above the roofing slabs, there are a series of rough-hewn granite blocks, which contain five compartments. The space above the *"King's" Room* was named *Davison's Room,* after its discoverer Nathanael Davison.

Δ   Some thought that this particular roof design was prob-

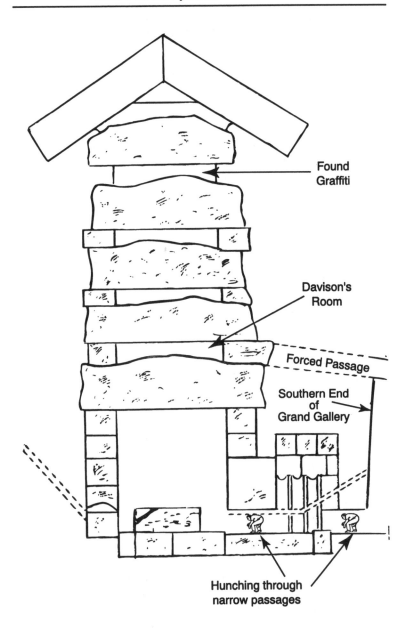

Found
Graffiti

Davison's
Room

Forced Passage

Southern End
of
Grand Gallery

Hunching through
narrow passages

The "King's" Room

ably made to reduce the pressure from the colossal weight of the stone above.

This theory is not convincing because the lower "Queen's" Room is subject to greater stress, yet it does not have this roof design.

Δ   On one of the upper slabs is some graffitti with the name of **Khufu**. This is the only reference to **Khufu** inside the pyramid. It is even questionable if such graffiti was carved during **Khufu**'s era or by a modern-day visitor. The pyramid is totally void of any official inscriptions.

•   •   •

Δ   At the western end of the room is the mysterious empty, lidless chest, made of very smooth granite. No inscription on it whatsoever.

Δ   The granite chest has been badly damaged by souvenir hunters, chipping pieces from its edges.

Did this granite chest hold the king's mummy?

The answer is *NO,* because:

1.   The passageway into the room is too narrow to pass this granite chest.
     Therefore, it had to have been placed in the room, as the pyramid was being built, contrary to the normal burial custom, practiced by the ancient Egyptians.

2.   There is not the slightest evidence of a corpse having been in this room, not a sign of funerary material or fragment of any artifact.
     No clue, however miniscule, has ever been found in this room or anywhere else in the Great Pyramid, to indicate that a burial took place here.

Empty, uninscribed,
lidless granite chest

Entrance to room is smaller
than granite chest

The "King's" Room

3.   Notwithstanding all other reasons, if we assume for a moment that this room was used for the dead Pharaoh's mummy, then they must have placed this oversized granite chest in the room during the construction of the pyramid. Then when the King died, they must have dragged his dead body up these difficult passages, and squeezed his dead body through the narrow constrictions, to place the mummy into the uninscribed granite chest.

That does not make any sense.

If people look at all these physical facts, it becomes quite obvious that the tomb theory is insulting to our intelligence.

Where is the lid for this granite chest?

Not even a portion of a lid was ever found in any of the pyramid passages or rooms.

Hypothetically, if we assume that the robbers made it to this room to steal the contents, they might have smashed the lid but they would hardly have taken the trouble to steal a broken lid. In spite of careful search, no chips of a broken granite lid have been found anywhere in the pyramid passages or rooms.

You have mentioned the Arabs' traditions with women's burial rooms earlier. Did the Arabs name this room too?

Yes, the Arabs named it this way because it reminded them of their tombs for men. Arabs buried their men in tombs with flat roofs, and this room has a flat roof. Ergo, this room was labeled the *"King's" Room* for its flat roof. No other reason.

The walls and the granite chest are and always were totally void of any inscriptions.

This room is simple yet powerful. Is there any significance to the design layout of this room?

Actually there is. The most obvious significance is that its configuration/proportion emphasizes the importance of volume in Egypt's architecture.

The floor plan of the room is a double square (2 x 1 rectangle), 20 x 10 Egyptian cubits (34'-4" x 17'-2", 10.5 x 5.2m).

The double square, divided by a single diagonal CA, forms two right triangles, each having a base of 1 and a height of 2. The diagonal CA is equal to the square root of 5 (2.236), i.e. 22.36 cubits in actual length.

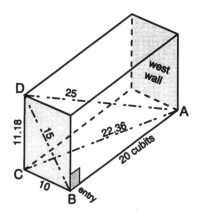

The height of the room is designed to be one half the length of the floor diagonal CA, i.e. $\sqrt{5}/2$, which is 11.18 cubits (19'-2" or 5.8m) in actual length.

This choice of CD, as the height of the room, will make the diagonal DB (in the triangle DCB) equal to 15 cubits. The result is that the three sides of the triangle ABD are in relation to 3:4:5.

The harmonic proportion of this room shows the intimate relationship between 1 : 2 : 3 : 4 : 5, and demonstrates the relationship in the divine harmonic proportion *(sacred geometry)* between process and structure. It also shows that the right-angle triangle principle (so-called *Pythagoras*) was practiced in the Egyptian design regularly, 2,000 years before Pythagoras walked this earth.

• • •

Attention is drawn to the holes in the north and south walls. (*see opposite page*)

Are these the channels that they call "air shafts"?

Δ   Yes. These channels have the same configuration as the ones in the *"Queen's" Room*, i.e. approximately 8" x 8" (20cm x 20cm).

Δ   Both channels, here, emerge on the exterior of the pyramid, unlike the channels in the *"Queen's" Room*, which do not go all the way through the exterior.

How can some people think that these channels were installed for the ventilation of a burial vault, if this was a burial room?

Both inclined channels start about 3' (1m) above floor level, where a vent logically starts at the ceiling level by running them through one horizontal course. There is no need to have two inclined shafts running through all the courses of the pyramid.

How about Egyptian tombs all over Egypt, do any of them have similar channels?

None whatsoever, and nobody expects them to ventilate their tombs.

How about the other pyramids, do any of them have similar channels?

None of the other pyramids have such channels.

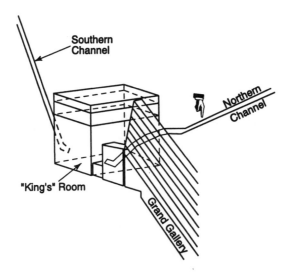

Kink in Northern Channel

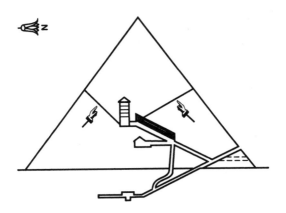

Orientation of the two channels in the "King's" Room

19

Abu Rawash

Pyramid #8
Gedefra's Pyramid

Next, we travel to ABU RAWASH, which is 5 miles (8 km) northwest of Giza.

Here, we will visit Pyramid #8.

What is at Abu Rawash?

At Abu Rawash, we find the pyramid that was attributed to Khufu's successor, Gedefra, who reigned from 2528-2520 BCE.

The pyramid is built in a curiously desolate and lonely site. It is located on a steep rock, more than 490' (150m) above the Nile Valley. This is a really difficult and inaccessible location.

•   •   •

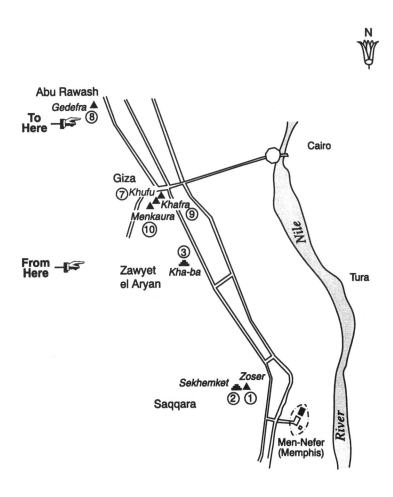

Map of the Ten Pyramids (Partial)

Upon arriving to the site, one sees a pitiful heap of rubble.

What happened to this pyramid?

Δ   As with many ancient Egyptian monuments, it was destroyed by the invading Arabs.

Δ   When it was complete, it was much smaller than Khufu's pyramid. Actually it is even smaller than the first Step Pyramid of Zoser.

This is a sudden change from the Great Pyramid of Khufu.

It appears to us that way, but it is not the case. Khufu did not build a personal monument. He did not leave any markings on it to give credit to himself. Khufu built a pyramid, and Gedefra built another pyramid, all as part of a master plan.

This desolate location is curious.

It is the most northerly of all the masonry pyramids, and is located about the same distance from Saqqara as the Meidum Pyramid (the most southerly) is located from Saqqara.

What is underneath it?

Δ   There is the typical 1:2 diagonal passage on its northern side.

Δ   The descending passage is about 27' (8m) wide but not very high, just like the other previous pyramids. It is 157' (48m) long.

Δ   There is one empty room, at the bottom of a wide shaft.

Δ   There is no inscription anywhere inside or outside the pyramid.

Present Height:	40' (12m)
Base:	320' square (100m)

The Remainder of Gedefra's Pyramid

Giza

Pyramid #9
Khafra's Pyramid
The Exterior

Next, we will go back to GIZA, which is 5 miles (8 km) southeast of ABU RAWASH. Here, we will discuss Pyramid #9 and Pyramid #10.

(Location map on page 23)

Who built this pyramid?

Khafra (Chephren in Greek), who succeeded Gedefra and reigned from 2520-2494 BCE, is credited with building this pyramid. Like all the other masonry pyramids, after Zoser's, it is essentially anonymous.

What is the evidence that this pyramid was built during Khafra's reign?

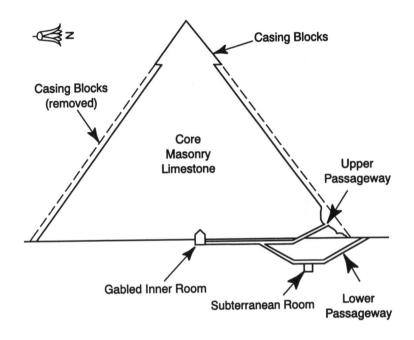

Height:	471' (143.5m)
Base:	708' square (214.5m)
	[error from true north 5'-30"]
Mass:	5.3 million tons
Inclination Angle:	53° 07' 48"

Khafra's Pyramid

The attribution is made through Herodotus' account, and the surrounding funerary complex, which repeatedly makes reference to his name. There are no inscriptions in the pyramid.

I know that this pyramid is smaller than Khufu's. But why does it look bigger to me?

It looks bigger to everybody because:

1 - It was built on a slightly higher ground than Khufu's.

2 - It maintained its summit, while Khufu's pyramid lost its top 33' (10m).

As it is the most preserved pyramid of the Giza group, it stands close to Khufu's and in size is almost its twin.

I notice an outcrop of local stone, to the south and west of this pyramid.

This is true, since the original ground was sloping in this area. The ancient Egyptians had to cut from two sides and fill the lower parts on the other two sides, in order to make the base absolutely level.

So, we can really see here the conditions of the local limestone.

Exactly. And as you can see, it is very fragile, full of strata and fault lines.

Just by looking at the perfect condition of the pyramid blocks, and comparing it to the exposed natural rock onsite, it is easy to conclude that the blocks could never have come from local sources.

How about the stone block sizes here?

Just like Khufu's pyramid, the heights of the blocks here are staggered, but they all have the same width.

Uniform width of blocks is another indication that they were molded. Right?

Exactly. Also, Dr. Joseph Davidovits, the chemist and Egyptologist, checked the 22 steps near the top, and found that they conform to 10 uniform lengths. Yet more strong evidence of the use of standard molding forms. Even if, hypothetically, we ignore the dire conditions of the natural limestone, the blocks could never have been quarried with such uniform lengths.

How about the casing blocks here?

Δ   The upper courses consist of fine-grained limestone casing blocks.

Δ   The lower courses consist of granite casing blocks.

Δ   The casing stones fit perfectly together with tongue and groove joints.

Δ   There are still a large number of the white limestone casing stones, on the upper courses.

How did they ever manage to install the casing stones without chipping the corners even slightly?

As we said before, you don't see any broken stones anywhere in the Giza Plateau. This again confirms that the pyramid blocks and casing stones were probably molded on site.

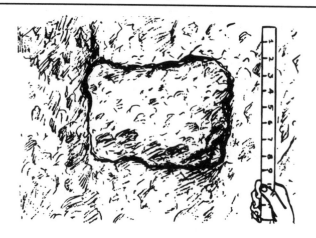

A large rubble stone em-
bedded in a stone block

It makes sense, but is there more evidence?

Let us look at some of these blocks. In some of them, you can see the outline of a stone incorporated into the block, which means that such blocks were cast and could not have been quarried.

•   •   •

Another piece of evidence for man-made stone are the huge paving blocks around the pyramids. One can clearly see these very durable, perfectly fitted, square angled blocks, each is several yards (meters) in length.

I see that they are joined together in such a beautiful strange mosaic.

Ancient Egyptians, throughout history, avoided the simple abrupt interlocking joints. Creating uninterrupted continuous corners allowed the energies to flow unimpeded.

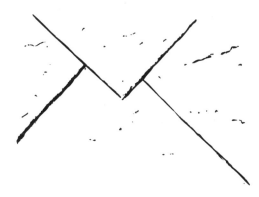

Huge paving blocks, located around the
pyramids, are perfectly fitted.

• • •

How about the geometry of this pyramid?

The triangular cross section of the pyramid of **Khafra**
(Chephren) is basically twin 3:4:5 triangles, side-by-side, where
the height would be 4 units to the base of 6.

Is the 3:4:5 triangle also called the "Pythagorian" Triangle?

Western academia calls it that, even though they have no
evidence to support their claim. This is yet another example
of intellectual piracy, since even Plutarch (46-120 CE), a Greek
historian himself, called it the **Ausar** (Osiris) Triangle.

This triangle, and other triangular shapes, has been used
and calculated in ancient Egyptian texts since, at least, the Pyramid Age, i.e. 3,000 years before Pythagoras walked this earth.

Δ   Δ   Δ

The Temples of Khafra

Since we are on the subject of the molding or quarrying question, let us go and check the large blocks at the Pyramid (erroniously known as *mortuary*) Temple and the Valley Temple of **Khafra**.

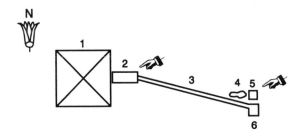

Profile of Causeway

1 Pyramid of Khafra.
2 Pyramid (erroneously known as *mortuary*) Temple of Khafra.
3 Causeway to Valley Temple.
4 Great Sphinx.
5 Temple of the Sphinx.
6 Valley Temple of Khafra.

Okay with me.

There is a lot to talk about this area, but let us just focus on the core limestone blocks, which were used to build these Temples.

Some of these huge coarse blocks weigh well over a hundred tons. A few

Wavy lift lines indicative of construction interruption during casting.

of them weigh up to 500 tons apiece. These huge blocks are very closely fitted.

Notice these wavy horizontal lines in them. If these blocks were quarried, they would show a straight line for different strata.

Why are these lines wavy and not horizontal?

The wavy line indicates that they stopped pouring the synthetic concrete for the day, or that a problem occured which caused work stoppage, for several hours.

When a huge block of concrete is cast, it takes more than a single day to complete the job.

This is too overwhelming. I can't argue the evidence. The evidence is all over!
To quarry and hoist these huge blocks and to set them so close to each other is unbelievable.

Is it more believable to have them cast on site?

Most definitely. How else can you have a perfect fit between 500 ton pieces of blocks?

Δ   Δ   Δ

The harmonic design layout of Khafra's Pyramid (erroneously called *mortuary*) Temple is discussed and shown in Chapter 7 of this book.

Δ   Δ   Δ

Khafra's Pyramid
The Interior

The internal structure of this pyramid is of extreme simplicity as compared to Khufu's pyramid.

Do we have two entrances here?

Yes. There are two entrances, one directly above the other, leading into the pyramid. The upper entrance, 50' (15m) above ground, is the typical entrance, and the one which we use to enter.

We walk into the narrow passage, which follows the diagonal of a 1:2 rectangle, down into the bedrock. It levels off, and then continues horizontally to a large limestone room.

The walls of the sloping section and part of the horizontal section are lined with red granite for unknown reasons.

The passages are again totally void of any inscriptions.

We enter the only room inside the pyramid.

This is a spacious room.

It is 46½' x 16½' x 22½' (14.2m x 5m x 6.9m). This room is hewn out of the rock, and roofed with gabled limestone

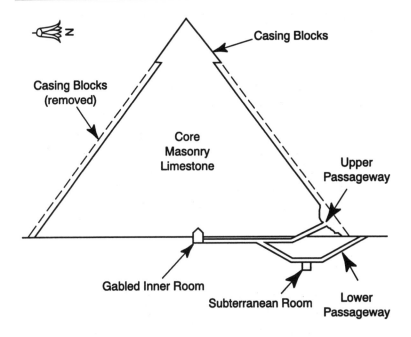

Interior of Khafra's Pyramid

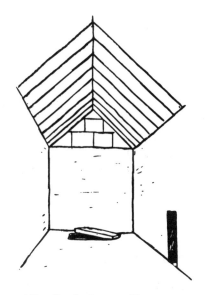

Khafra's Inner Room

slabs. These slabs are set at the same angle as the pyramid face.

Wow! So these gables are carrying the whole immense weight of the pyramid?

Yes. This simple gabled roof is adequate to support the whole weight of the pyramid above it. Remember the roof of the *"King's" Room* in Khufu's pyramid? What they call the relieving stones, above the *"King's" Room*, were not needed for structural purposes, because we can see here that a single gable above the flat ceiling would have sufficed structurally.

So, what they termed as "relieving stones", in the *"King's" Room* of Khufu's Pyramid, is not for structural purposes, but for other non-structural reasons, which we are unaware of.

Right.

●　　●　　●

At the far western end of this totally bare room, is an empty, uninscribed, beautiful, polished granite box 8.5' x 3.5' (2.6m x 1.05m), and 3.3' (1.0m) deep. This box is set into the floor of the room, up to the level of the lid. The lid, broken in two pieces, lies nearby.

Who broke the lid, and placed it there?

Nobody knows, but that is how the Italian adventurer, Belzoni, found it when he first entered this pyramid in 1818.

Did Belzoni find a mummy or any sign of a funeral?

None whatsoever. There is no evidence whatsoever that Khafra or anyone else was ever buried in the stone chest, embedded in the main room.

• • •

Let us go outside the pyramid again, and look at the lower entrance.

What do we have here?

The entrance here is entirely hewn into the bedrock. At the bottom of this passageway, there is a large, empty, uninscribed subterranean room.

What was this subterranean room, and all these passages for?

Nobody knows. But you know what they say when they can't figure it out.

Wait, let me guess. The usual explanation, "Change in Plan."

Exactly. Their usual escape route for hard to explain matters.

Δ   Δ   Δ

Pyramid #10
Menkaura's Pyramid
The Exterior

Then we walk to the third pyramid of Giza, which is attributed to Menkaura (Mycerinus in Greek), who reigned from 2494-2472 BCE.

So, this pyramid, like the other nine pyramids, is anonymous.

That is right — no inscriptions anywhere. Only the account of Herodotus, and references to his name in the surrounding mastabas, make him the likely builder.

This is much smaller than the other two pyramids of Khufu and Khafra.

This pyramid is only 7% of the size of Khufu's pyramid, even though Menkaura reigned for 18 years, and had plenty of time to finish a pyramid as big as Khufu's or Khafra's.

Yet, this small (and last stone) pyramid is the most harmonious of them all. It was the last of the series.

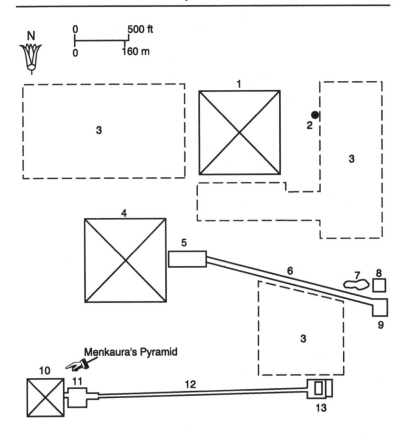

1 Great Pyramid of Khufu (Cheops).
2 Tomb of Hetepheres.
3 Mastaba Fields.
4 Pyramid of Khafra (Chephren).
5 Pyramid Temple of Khafra.
6 Causeway to Valley Temple.
7 Great Sphinx.
8 Temple of the Sphinx.
9 Valley Temple of Khafra.
10 Pyramid of Menkaura (Mycerinus).
11 Pyramid Temple of Menkaura.
12 Menkaura Causeway.
13 Valley Temple of Menkaura.

Giza Plateau

Why didn't he build a larger pyramid?

Δ   The size was not his objective. These are not personal monuments. His pyramid is just a piece of the master plan, centered in Saqqara.

•   •   •

The casing blocks here are different than the other two Giza pyramids.

The lower half of the casing blocks are made of rough granite (possibly carved from natural quarries), except at the northern face of the pyramid, around the entrance and in a corresponding area on the eastern face, where they are fine granite.

How about the top half of the casing blocks?

The top half of the pyramid was fully dressed with the fine-grained limestone, but the Arabs destroyed them.

In 1196 CE, one of the Moslem rulers of Egypt tried to destroy this pyramid but had to stop because of the great expense.

•   •   •

What makes this pyramid so pleasant?

The 12th century Iraqi physician, Abdul Latif, made a special note of this in his book, *The Eastern Sky*:

The last one appears small compared with the other two, but viewed at a short distance and to the exclusion of these it excites in the imagination a singular oppression, and cannot be contemplated without painfully affecting the sight.

Notwithstanding Abdul Latif's expression (or poor English translation), the point is that there is almost unanimous agreement that the pyramid produces an effect of concentrated *power.*

With such effects, the design must have conformed to subtle sacred and harmonious proportions.

Exactly. It is not its size, but its proportions that overwhelm us. Although it is the smallest and youngest of the three pyramids on the Giza Plateau, it has the most interesting harmonic design. Its cross section is very nearly an 5:8 triangle, representing the Neb (Golden) Proportion (also see Chapter 7).

Additionally, the ratio of the height to half the diagonal would be 8:9 (the perfect musical tone), with an angle between the edge and the horizontal of 51° 29' 53".

Wow! No wonder it is so appealing to our senses.

Yes, it is the perfect application of harmonic proportion (commonly known as *sacred geometry*).

This pyramid signified the end of the Pyramid Age.

What a beautiful ending.

Δ   Δ   Δ

Pyramid #10
Menkaura's Pyramid
The Interior

How about the interior here?

The passageways here are very different from Khufu's and Khafra's.

There are two passageways:

1. The upper passageway has its entrance, as usual, on the northern face of the pyramid, and its entrance is 13' (4m) above the base of the pyramid. This descending passage is the typical diagonal of a 1:2 rectangle, measuring about 102' (31m). The sloping section leads into a horizontal passage, which in turn, leads into the first inner room.

2. The second passageway is cut underneath the original upper passageway. The lower passageway is the one we use to enter the pyramid and it is lined with granite. It also, as usual, follows the slope of the diagonal of a 1:2 rectangle. The lower passage leads westward to a staircase, then down to a room containing six niches (called the *Celled Room*). Still further west, lies the main underground room.

Why was the passageway lined with granite, since it was in the bedrock?

We can't explain this feature, at this time.

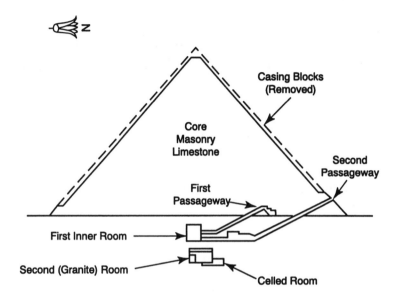

Base: 356' square (108m) [error from true north = 14"]
Height: 218' (67m)
Mass: 0.6 million tons
Slope: (face to base) 51° 20' 25" (5/4)
        (edge to base) 51° 29' 53" (8/9)

Cross section of Menkaura's Pyramid

How about the main underground room?

It is cut out of the bedrock, and again, it is entirely lined with red granite and totally void of any inscriptions.

Its ceiling appears to be vaulted — a perfect barrel vault — but on closer examination, you will find that the ceiling is actually formed of large, tightly fitted granite slabs, laid in facing gables. The undersides have been carved to form the false vault.

Was this granite room always empty like it is now?

No. This room contained the only stone chest found in this pyramid. It is a basalt chest, with no inscriptions whatsoever.

I have not seen it. What happened to it?

It was carried out earlier this century, to be shipped to England, but was lost at sea, off the Spanish coast.

Δ   Δ   Δ

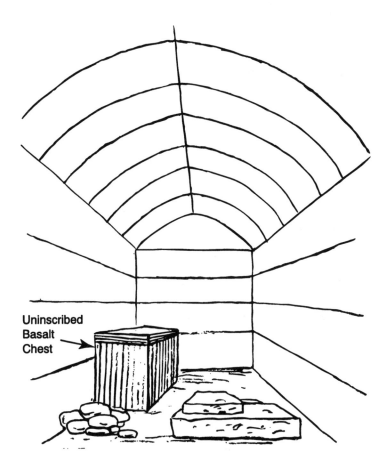

Uninscribed
Basalt
Chest

Main Underground Room in Menkaura's Pyramid

EPILOGUE

The End of the Pyramid Age

So the last genuine pyramid was the relatively small pyramid of Menkaura. Who reigned after Menkaura?

Shepseskaf (2472-2467 BCE) followed **Menkaura**. He did not build a pyramid or a mastaba. Instead, he built a different type of a royal monument. It was in the shape of a rectangular sarcophagus, 328' x 236' x 66' (100m x 72m x 20m). Arabs called it *Mastabat Fara-un*.

Other features of this monument are:

1. It did not include any inscriptions whatsoever, and no direct reference to Shepseskaf. References to him are made in nearby tombs.

2. The passage to the underground room follows the typical diagonal of a 1:2 rectangle.

3. It was never used for Shepsekaf's burial.

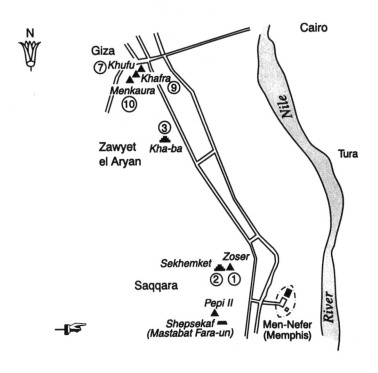

Map of the Ten Pyramids (Partial)

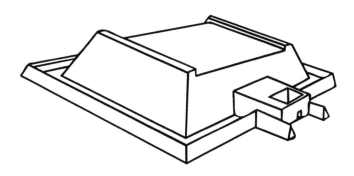

A reconstruction of Mastabat Fara'un

What happened? What made them stop building masonry pyramids?

The objective of building the pyramids, as structures to attract and channel cosmic energy, had been completed.

We subconsciously continue to think that the pyramids were personal monuments (which they were not). It is therefore that we have difficulty understanding why they stopped. They did not just stop. The job was complete.

Δ   Δ   Δ

The Endless Journey

Your journey to visit all the genuine masonry pyramids and some of the ungenuine rubble pyramids has ended. You have all the basic facts. Many, but not all, of your concerns have been addressed.

The search for the truth never ends. For as we know more, we find out that there is more to learn.

As you travel on this grander journey, keep in mind the following tips:

Δ   Not knowing the reason for certain things does not give us the license to speculate and fabricate answers, thereby corrupting history. We just have to keep looking and trying to find the correct answers.

Δ   Because you are not an "expert" in a particular field, it does not mean that you have to accept or be intimidated by other so-called "experts". Let logic, reason and unbias guide you toward the truth. As you wade through the various views, keep in mind Sir William Oster's words: *"The greater the ignorance, the greater the dogmatism!"*

Enjoy your journey.

Glossary

BCE - <u>B</u>efore <u>C</u>ommon <u>E</u>ra. Noted in many references as BC.

Canopic Jars - special jars used to store the vital organs of the deceased. The jars were placed in the tomb chamber near the mummy. The jars had lids shaped after the heads of the four sons of Heru(*Horus*), who were in charge of the protection and/or progression of the viscera. Each of the four sons was himself under the protection of a netert, and each was associated with one of the cardinal points.

CE - <u>C</u>ommon <u>E</u>ra. Noted in many references as AD.

Circle Index - designates the ratio of the circumference of a circle to its diameter, and is equal to 22/7.

concrete - a building material made of sand and gravel, bonded together with cement, into a hard, compact substance.

cubit - The ancient Egyptian unit of linear measurement, which is the distance between the elbow and the tip of the extended middle finger.
   one cubit   = 1.72' (0.5236m)

Heb-Sed - ancient festival associated with the rejuvenation and spiritual and physical renewal of the Pharaoh.

Khnum - ram-headed patron of Elephantine (the Cataract region) and of Esna. Khnum molded man from clay, on a potter's wheel.

mastaba - the Arabic word for *bench*; a mud-brick, aboveground structure. The burial chambers of the deceased are found below the mastaba.

mummification - the process was basically one of dehydration of the body, after the removal of the brain (through the nostrils), and the viscera (through an incision in the side of the body). The body is then packed with temporary material containing dehydrating and preserving agents, for forty days. The temporary packing is then replaced with permanent resin-soaked linens and fragrances. The body is then anointed and wrapped in fine linen gauze. It took seventy days to complete the process.

Neb (Golden) Proportion - is the *"key to the structure of the cosmos"*. It is obtained using a rectangle of sides 1:2. If an approximation must be made, its value is 1.6180339. . . .

Phi - (ϕ), *see* Neb (Golden) Proportion.

Pi - (π), *see* Circle Index.

Ptah - great creator **neter** (god) of **Men-Nefer** (Memphis), the architect of heaven and earth. Patron of craftsmen, equated by the Greeks to Hephaestus.

pyramid - a solid figure having a polygonal base, the sides of which form the bases of triangular surfaces meeting at a common vertex.

Pyramid Texts - A collection of funerary literature that was found in the tombs of the Kings of the 5th and 6th Dynasties (2465-2150 BCE). *(see pages 25-26)*

Seker - hawk-headed, with a swathed male figure; represents the deepest stage of the sun's journey beneath the earth (**Duat**). Saqqara is probably named after Seker.

slope - the amount or degree of the deviation from the horizontal or vertical in an inclined surface. The ratio of the vertical difference divided by the horizontal difference.

Selected Bibliography

Aldred, C. *Egypt to the End of the Old Kingdom*. London, 1965.

Alvarez, L. W. *et al*. Search for Hidden Chambers in the Pyramids. *Science* 167 (1970)

Badawy, Alexander. *Ancient Egyptian Architectural Design*. Los Angeles, CA, USA, 1965.

Badawy, A. 'The Stellar Destiny of Pharaoh and the so-called Air-shafts in Cheops's Pyramid', in *MIOAWB*, band 10, 1964

Breasted, J. H. *History of Egypt*. Chicago, 1919.

Brecher, K. and Feirtag, M. *Astronomy of the Ancients*. Mass., 1979 ed.

Clarke, S. and Engelbach, R. *Ancient Egyptian Masonry*. Oxford, 1930.

Cornell, J. *The First Stargazers, An Introduction to the Origins of Astronomy*. London, 1981.

Davidovits, Dr. Joseph and Morris, Margie. *The Pyramids, An Enigma Solved*. New York, 1989.

De Cenival, Jean-Louis. *Living Architecture*. New York, 1964.

Edwards, I. E. S. *The Pyramids of Egypt*. Rev. ed. Harmondsworth, 1961; and London, 1972.

Erman, Adolf. *Life in Ancient Egypt*. New York, 1971.

Fakhry, Ahmed. *The Pyramids*. Chicago, 1969.

Firth, C. M., Quibell, J. E. and Lauer, J.-P. *The Step Pyramid*. 2 vols. Cairo, 1935-36.

Gadalla, Moustafa. *Historical Deception, The Untold Story of Ancient Egypt - Second Edition*. Greensboro, NC, U.S.A., 1999.

Gadalla, Moustafa. *Egyptian Cosmology: The Absolute Harmony*. Greensboro, NC, USA, 1997.

Gadalla, Moustafa. *Exiled Egyptians: The Heart of Africa*. Greensboro, NC, USA, 1999.

Gardner, Martin. *The Magic Numbers of Dr. Matrix*. New York, 1985.

Grinsell, L. *Egyptian Pyramids*. Gloucester, 1947.

Herodotus. *The Histories*, tr. A. de Selincourt. New York, 1954.

Internet - Information from websites.

James, T. G. H. *An Introduction to Ancient Egypt*. London, 1979.

Lauer, J-P. *Le Probleme des Pyramides d' Egypte*. Paris, 1948.

Lemesurier, Peter. *The Great Pyramid Decoded*. New York, 1977.

Mendelssohn, Kurt. *The Riddle of the Pyramid*. New York, 1974.

Murray, Margaret A. *The Splendour that was Egypt*. New York, 1957.

Pennick, Nigel. *Sacred Geometry*. New York, 1982.

Petrie, W. M. F. *The Pyramids and Temples of Gizeh.* London, 1883.

Smyth, Piazza. *The Great Pyramid, Its Secrets and Mysteries Revealed.* London, 1880.

Stewart, Desmond. *The Pyramids and the Sphinx, Egypt Under the Pharaohs.* New York, 1977.

Tompkins, Peter. *Secrets of the Great Pyramid.* New York, 1971.

Trimble, V. 'Astronomical Investigations concerning the so-called Air-shafts of Cheops's Pyramid', in *JEA*, 21; 1936.

West, John Anthony. *The Travelers Key to Ancient Egypt.* New York, 1989.

Wilkinson, Sir J. Gardner. *The Ancient Egyptians, Their Life and Customs.* London, 1988.

Numerous references written in Arabic.

Sources and Notes

In my research, I came across dozens of books. Many of them are commercially oriented towards selling at any cost. I don't dignify such books by listing them even though they sell very well.

This book represents my interpretations from various sources. I believe that a researcher should not be content with referring to a single (or a few) references to support a point. It is my belief that to search for the truth, several sources must be considered and evaluated, and pieces of evidence must be put together like pieces of a puzzle, in the right location and time. A single reference may (and often does) intentionally or unintentionally leave out something, or color it.

Almost all my sources are written by very biased authors, who (consciously or sub-consciously) have pro-Western and/ or Judeo-Christian paradigms.

My references to the sources are listed in the previous section, **Selected Bibliography**. They are only referred to for the facts, events, and dates, and not necessarily for their interpretations of such information.

Chapter 2 (Tombs)

Information on tombs, contents, and functions were obtained from: Erman, Gadalla, James, West, Wilkinson.

The difference between the Egyptian pyramids and tombs were obtained from Gadalla, Mendelssohn, and West.

Mendelssohn provided the most convincing points that destroy the academicians' "tomb theory". Other than that, the rest of the book is unfounded grandstanding and speculation.

Chapter 3 (Genuine Pyr.)

Primary Sources: Davidovits, Fakhry, Mendelssohn, Petrie, and West.

Secondary Sources: All other listed references.

Chapter 4 (Pyramid Texts)

Primary Sources: Practically all listed references.

Chapter 5 (Construction Techniques)

The Common Theory
Practically all listed references.

Egyptian Know-How
Primary Sources: Davidovits, Firth (,Quibell & Lauer), Gadalla (*Historical Deception*), West, and Wilkinson.
Secondary Sources: Other listed references.

Sources of Stones
Primary Sources: Davidovits.
Davidovits, who is an expert in geopolymer and concrete technology, was very methodical in his presentation of

facts related to the material and construction techniques. However, he was very careless in writing about historical and religious aspects of ancient Egypt. He did not hesitate to speculate in those areas without any evidence.

It should be noted that the author is a graduate civil engineer, 1967, and has practiced civil engineering ever since. The author endorses Davidovits' findings, in the areas of natural and man-made blocks, based on his knowledge of the technical subject matter, and his numerous examinations of the Egyptian monuments.

Synthetic and Natural Blocks
Primary Sources: Alvarez and Davidovits.

It should be noted that the author is a graduate civil engineer, 1967, and has practiced civil engineering ever since. The author endorses Davidovits' findings, in this particular area, based on his knowledge of the technical subject matter, and his numerous examinations of the Egyptian monuments.

Casing Stones
Primary Sources: Davidovits and West.
Secondary Sources: Practically all other listed references.

Fictional Ramps
Primary Sources: Davidovits and West.

Abandonment
Primary Source: West
Secondary Sources: Practically all other listed references.

Chapter 6 (Pyramid Power)

Primary Sources: Gardner and West.

Chapter 7 (Harmonic)

Badawy (*Ancient Egyptian Architectural Design*), De Cenival, Gardner, Herodotus, Pennick, and West.

Chapter 8 thru 10 (Saqqara...)

General
Primary Sources: Badawy (*Ancient Egyptian Architectural Design*), Clarke, De Cenival, Edwards, Fakhry, Firth (,Quibell and Lauer), Grinsell, James, Lauer, Mendelssohn, Pennick, and West.

Chapter 11 (Sekhemket)

Sources: Davidovits, Fakhry, Mendelssohn, and Wilkinson.

Chapter 12 (Kha-ba)

Sources: Davidovits, Fakhry, and Mendelssohn.

Chapter 13 (Meidum)

Primary sources: Badawy (*Ancient Egyptian Architectural Design*), Davidovits, De Cenival, Fakhry, Lauer, Mendelssohn, Pennick, and West.
Secondary Sources: All other listed references.

Chapter 14 (Dahshur - Bent)

Primary Sources: Badawy (*Ancient Egyptian Architectural Design*), Davidovits, De Cenival, Fakhry, Lauer, Mendelssohn, Pennick, and West.

Secondary Sources: All other listed references.

Chapter 15 (Dahshur - Red)

Primary Sources: Badawy (*Ancient Egyptian Architectural Design*), Davidovits, De Cenival, Fakhry, Lauer, Mendelssohn, Pennick, and West.

Secondary Sources: All other listed references.

Chapter 16 (Ungenuine - Dahshur)

Sources: Practically all listed sources.

Chapter 17 (Giza Plateau)

Sources: Practically all listed sources.

Chapter 18 (Khufu)

Khufu - Exterior

Sources: Practically all listed sources.

For the harmonic proportion (sacred geometry) aspects: Badawy (*Ancient Egyptian Architectural Design*), De Cenival, Gardner, and West.

Khufu - Interior

Primary Sources: Smyth and West.
Secondary Sources: Practically all other listed references.

Chapter 19 (*Gedefra*)

Sources: Davidovits, Fakhry, and Mendelssohn.

Chapter 20 (Khafra)

Khafra - Exterior

Configuration:
    Primary: Davidovits, Fakhry, Lauer, and West.
    Secondary: Practically all other listed references.

Construction : Davidovits (pyramid), West (paving blocks).

Harmonic Proportion (Sacred Geometry): Badawy (*Ancient Egyptian Architectural Design*)

Khafra - Interior

Primary Sources: Fakhry and West.

Secondary Sources: Practically all other listed references.

Chapter 21 (Menkaura)

Menkaura - Exterior

Configuration:
Primary: Davidovits, Fakhry, Lauer, and West.
Secondary: Practically all other listed references.

Construction: Davidovits (pyramid), West (paving blocks).

Harmonic Proportion (Sacred Geometry): Badawy (*Ancient Egyptian Architectural Design*)

Menkaura - Interior

Primary Sources: Fakhry and West.

Secondary Sources: Practically all other listed references.

Chapter 22

Primary Sources: Davidovits and West.

Secondary Sources: Practically all other listed references.

Index

Tehuti Research Foundation

Tehuti Research Foundation (T.R.F.) is a non-profit, international organization, dedicated to ancient Egyptian studies. Our books are engaging, factual, well researched, practical, interesting, and appealing to the general public.

The books listed below are authored by T.R.F. chairman, Moustafa Gadalla.

Visit our website at:

http://www.egypt-tehuti.org
E-mail address: mgadalla@egypt-tehuti.org

About Our Books

Egyptian Harmony: The Visual Music
ISBN: 0-9652509-8-9 (pbk.), 192 pages, US$11.95

This book reveals the ancient Egyptian incredible and comprehensive knowledge of harmonic proportion, sacred geometry, music, and number mysticism, as manifested in their texts, temples, tombs, ...etc., throughout their dynastic history. Discover how the Word (sound) that created the World (forms) was likewise transformed to visual music by the Egyptians into hieroglyphs, art, and architecture. The book surveys the ancient Egyptian harmonic proportional application in all aspects of their civilization.

Historical Deception
The Untold Story of Ancient Egypt - Second Edition
ISBN: 0-9652509-2-X (pbk.), 352 pages, US$19.95

This book reveals the ingrained prejudices against ancient

Egypt, from both the religious groups, who deny that Egypt is the source of their creed, and Western rationalists, who deny the existence of science and philosophy prior to the Greeks. The book contains 46 chapters, with many interesting topics, such as the Egyptian medical knowledge about determining the sex of the unborn, and much, much more.

Exiled Egyptians: The Heart of Africa
ISBN: 0-9652509-6-2 (pbk.), 352 pages, US$19.95

Read about the forgotten ancient Egyptians, who fled the foreign invasions and religious oppressions, and rebuilt the ancient Egyptian model system in Africa, when Egypt itself became an Arab colony. Find out how a thousand years of Islamic jihads have fragmented and dispersed the African continent into endless misery and chaos. Discover the true causes and dynamics of the history of African slavery. Understand the genius of the ancient Egyptian/African religious, social, economical, and political systems.

Egyptian Cosmology: The Absolute Harmony
ISBN: 0-9652509-1-1 (pbk.), 160 pages, US$9.95

Discover the remarkably advanced Egyptian cosmology, which continues to be the Ancient Future of mankind and the universe. It is the ONLY metaphysics of all (ancient and modern) that is coherent, comprehensive, consistent, logical, analytical, and rational. This book is informative and well written, so that the whole spectrum of readers, from the casual to the serious, will find the subjects enlightening. The book surveys the applicability of Egyptian concepts to our modern understanding of the nature of the universe, creation, science, and philosophy, such as the Big Bang, and their enduring cosmic consciousness that All is One and One is All.

Tut-Ankh-Amen: The Living Image of the Lord
ISBN: 0-9652509-9-7 (pbk.), 144 pages, US$9.50

This book provides the overwhelming evidence from archeology, the Dead Sea Scrolls, the Talmud, and the Bible itself, that Tut-Ankh-Amen was the historical character of Jesus. The book examines the details of Tut's birth, life, death, resurrection, family roots, religion, teachings, etc., which were duplicated in the biblical account of Jesus. The book also reveals the world's greatest conspiracy and cover-up, which recreated the character of Jesus, living in another time (Roman era) and another place (Palestine/Israel).

Egypt: A Practical Guide
ISBN: 0-9652509-3-0 (pbk.), 256 pages, US$8.50

Experience Egypt! From the lively Nile Valley, to the solitary deserts, to the diverse Sinai, to the lush oases, to the exotic underwater life of the Red Sea, to the Mediterranean beaches. A no-nonsense, no-clutter, practical guide to Egypt, written by an Egyptian-American Egyptologist. Quick, easy, and comprehensive reference to sites of antiquities and recreation. Find your way with numerous maps and illustrations. Tips to understanding both the modern and ancient Egyptian cultures. Informative, detailed, and illustrated glossary.

Tehuti Research Foundation

Ordering Information

Name_____

Address_____

City_____

State/Province_____ _____

Country _____Tel. (____) _____

_____ Books @ $11.95 (Egyptian Harmony)   = $
_____ Books @ $19.95 (Historical Deception) = $
_____ Books @ $11.95 (Pyramid Handbook)   = $
_____ Books @ $ 9.50 (Tut-Ankh-Amen)   = $
_____ Books @ $ 9.95 (Egyptian Cosmology)   = $
_____ Books @ $ 8.50 (Egypt: Practical Guide) = $
_____ Books @ $19.95 (Exiled Egyptians)   = $_____
                          Subtotal   = $

North Carolina residents, add 6% Sales Tax   = $
Shipping: (N. America only) $2.00 for 1st book = $
          for each additional book $1 x _____   = $
Outside N. Amer. (per weight/destination)   = $_____
                              Total   = $

Payment: [ ] Check (payable: Tehuti Research Foundation)
          [ ] Visa [ ] MasterCard [ ] Discover

Card Number: _____

Name on Card: _____ Exp. Date: ___/___

Tehuti Research Foundation
P.O. Box 39406
Greensboro, NC   27438-9406   U.S.A.
Call TOLL FREE (North America) and order now 888-826-7021
Or FAX your order   212-656-1460
e-mail: info@egypt-tehuti.org